*Primer on Biblical Methods* is the work of a master teacher. Corrine Carvalho's book is not only thorough, moving all the way from source to postmodern criticism, but blessedly clear. Examples, questions, and exercises ensure that the reader understands each section. This work will be helpful for students approaching the complexity of biblical interpretation for the first time and also for professors who have been searching for ways to explain the intricacies of our task with clarity and simplicity.

Irene Nowell, OSB, PhD
a Benedictine of Mount St. Scholastica
Atchison, Kansas

I have been looking for something like this book for years. In the past it has been necessary to cobble together a packet of articles so that students would have access to information about various approaches to reading and interpreting the Bible. The beauty of this book is that it puts all these things into one book that will be read and reread, consulted and cross-referenced.

Carvalho's familiarity with questions asked by today's students enhances the *Primer on Biblical Methods*. Not only does she address these questions, she incorporates examples from a contemporary perspective in a lively and engaging manner. Students don't have to pick up a heavy tome and plow through unnecessary technical terminology. Carvalho turns exotic terminology into interesting stuff! It is a model of engaging erudition.

Chris Franke
Professor of Hebrew Bible/Old Testament
St. Catherine University, St. Paul, MN

## AUTHOR ACKNOWLEDGMENTS

I would like to thank my many students over the years. They have challenged me to forget the jargon and just tell them what I mean. They have shown me by their excitement that methods matter, and they remind me every day that biblical studies must address them in their world before we can ask them to enter someone else's. This book is for them.

# PRIMER ON
# BIBLICAL METHODS

CORRINE L. CARVALHO, PhD

ANSELM ACADEMIC

Created by the publishing team of Anselm Academic.

Cover image: *Biblia latina* (Bible in Latin). England, thirteenth century. Manuscript on vellum. Lessing J. Rosenwald Collection, Rare Book and Special Collections Division, Library of Congress.

The scriptural quotations contained herein are from the New Revised Standard Version of the Bible, Catholic Edition. Copyright © 1993 and 1989 by the Division of Christian Education of the National Council of the Churches of Christ in the United States of America. All rights reserved.

Printed in the United States of America

7025

ISBN 978-1-59982-015-6

Library of Congress Cataloging-in-Publication Data

Carvalho, Corrine L.
     Primer on biblical methods / Corrine L. Carvalho.
     p. cm.
Includes bibliographical references (p.    ) and index.
ISBN 978-1-59982-015-6 (pbk.)
     1. Bible—Hermeneutics. I. Title.
BS476.C317 2009
220.601—dc22

2009018952

# CONTENTS

# A QUICK GUIDE TO BIBLICAL INTERPRETATION

## FOREWORD FOR THE INSTRUCTOR

I teach theology in a Catholic university, primarily to students who are taking courses to fulfill general requirements. Typically they have little patience for obscure theories or arcane facts, but that doesn't mean they're not interested in theological questions. Spiritual questions are as important to them as they were to college students when I was their age. The problem is that many theological textbooks are not written to target this particular audience. Many of these students particularly want to know more about the Bible. So a couple of years ago, I wrote a textbook for use with my undergraduate students, *Encountering Ancient Voices: A Guide to Reading the Old Testament* (Anselm Academic, 2006).

Some professors who have considered using this textbook would prefer something a bit less comprehensive regarding the biblical text itself for the courses that they teach. Instead, they would rather supplement their lectures with a handbook that teaches students about modern methods of biblical interpretation. That is the purpose of this primer. Because this is not strictly an introductory textbook, it presumes that students have access to terms common in biblical studies, so it does not define some of the more common biblical vocabulary. If students are entirely novice to the enterprise of biblical studies, a glossary of biblical terms might be a handy adjunct to this text.

In the past I have used Daniel Harrington's *Interpreting the New Testament: A Practical Guide* and *Interpreting the Old Testament: A Practical Guide* (Michael Glazier, 1979 and 1981, respectively). These books are written in a clear, direct manner and give a blueprint students can follow. However, the books are also dated and do not include discussions of methods that probably speak most urgently to contemporary students, methods like feminist criticism or new historicism. This primer uses Harrington's books as a model, but expands the discussion to include these newer methods. Each chapter also includes brief exercises for students to practice each method, applying it to both Old and New Testament examples. Adaptability is a further virtue of this primer, as each chapter can stand alone, so that instructors can pick and choose the material most useful to them.

Where appropriate, I have also included some discussions of theological issues that students face in specifically Christian contexts. In addition, the final section of the book gives some examples of the history of Christian biblical interpretation. These include examples from Catholic theology, the context in which I teach, as well as from other Christian denominations; however, because of the brevity of this primer, these latter are necessarily limited.

This book is designed for beginners in biblical studies. My goal is to introduce them to the critical methods of biblical interpretation that will make them better readers of the text. I have tried to write a guide that both affirms the students' desire to learn more and gently challenges them to adopt more complex reading strategies that are better suited for our twenty-first-century world.

## FOREWORD FOR THE STUDENT

"Why can't we just read the plain meaning of the text?" a student asked. It was early in the spring semester a few years ago, and I was teaching an upper-division course on women in the Old Testament to students who were fulfilling their general education requirements. My questioner, a bright senior engineering major, just couldn't understand why we had to ask all these different questions about a text that to him was perfectly clear. Why make something as simple as the Bible so complicated? Fortunately, by the end of the course, this student realized how much he missed when he restricted his understanding of a text to his own initial conclusions based on a cursory reading.

This student asked out loud what many students silently wonder: why learn to ask systematic questions of a biblical text? The first and most important reason is that these methods of investigation make us better readers of *any* text, including the Bible. The methods discussed here developed out of the understanding of the ways all authors write and the way individuals and communities interpret that writing. These methods also provide scholars a common vocabulary and strategies for investigation and reporting about the meaning of a text.

In addition, understanding these methods of investigation helps students evaluate the claims made in the world today about biblical truth. One of the first exercises that I have my students do is to evaluate the claims made about the Bible from recent newspaper articles. I have never been at a loss to find such articles. Christianity, with its focus on the Bible, is a significant cultural force in much of the contemporary world, including of course the United States and Canada, but often the same students who are quite able to evaluate claims made about science or the economy are at a loss when it comes to evaluating claims made about the Bible. No educated person in the world today, especially in North America, should be so naïve when it comes to such claims.

The purpose of this primer, then, is to make students better readers of biblical texts. It teaches them a series of questions about the text that stem from what scholars call "critical" methods, not because these methods are critical of the truth claims of the Bible, but because they analyze and critique the data at hand.

After a general introduction that addresses theological issues, each section of this primer devotes itself to a different method or approach to interpreting the Bible. This handbook is divided into four parts. In the first part, I introduce methods designed to reconstruct some aspects of the text's production, or what some call "the world behind the text." Part 2 focuses on methods meant to draw out the meaning of the texts themselves, regardless of their production. Part 3 provides a guide to some of the contemporary reading communities that engage in biblical studies. This includes a discussion of explicitly theological readings. Part 4, which is devoted to an ever-growing interest in the history of biblical interpretation, provides some examples of important reading traditions that have shaped contemporary communities of faith.

Each section introduces individual methods. For each method I provide first a general introduction to the method, followed by its application within Old Testament studies and then within New Testament scholarship. As a summary for each method, I offer some questions typical of those asked by the method, as well as targeted exercises for applying the method.

## EXEGESIS AND BIBLICAL INTERPRETATION

Traditionally, guides to methods of biblical interpretation were designed to help seminary students write "exegesis papers," an exercise that is especially useful for those preparing to preach. Exegesis is the process of reading a text through the systematic application of a series of methods of biblical interpretation, with the purpose of arriving at an overall conclusion regarding the meaning of that text. The Greek word we translate as *exegesis* originally meant "to lead out," and it names the process of teasing out the meaning of a text. Its opposite is *eisigesis*, which is the process of reading *in* to a text meanings that are not properly there.

An exegesis paper focuses on drawing out the meaning of one particular biblical passage (often called a *pericope*). To practice exegesis, the student analyzes a text using a series of methods such as those described in this book. It was standard practice twenty years ago to assign students to do an exegesis, which teaches them the breadth of questions that can be asked of a text. Students practiced in exegesis are able to answer the question posed by my student: why do we need to do this? They have learned to uncover meanings in a text — meanings that are actually quite clear when looked at through a different lens.

While this book can be used as a guide for students who are writing an exegesis paper, it has other uses as well. Some of the most common resources for biblical studies are various biblical commentaries written by experts in the field. Different commentary series have different focuses, but they all tend to apply various methods of biblical interpretation systematically to a particular biblical book. It is impossible for students to harvest the treasures in these resources if they do not understand the questions the commentaries are meant to address.

Finally, even when my students do not write a classic exegesis paper, I insist that they read various opinions about the meaning of a text. They are always amazed by how many different interpretations of a text there are, and how their own interpretation can be changed by reading the viewpoints of others. A historical survey of marriage customs in the time of David is quite different from a feminist analysis of the story of David's marriage to Bathsheba. Yet both provide essential insights into 2 Samuel 11.

Many handbooks discuss these methods more fully, and I include a brief bibliography in this primer as well.

## THEOLOGY AND ANALYSIS: FRIENDS OR FOES?

Students at religiously affiliated universities often wonder about the relationship between critical study of the Bible and the way the Bible is proclaimed in a specific church. I find that this question is even more pressing for students who have had some religious education. What we do in a university classroom feels very different to them from the way they are used to hearing the Bible explained. Sometimes students conclude that the two approaches and the "meanings" they convey are simply incompatible, and that what they are learning in a classroom setting is wrong, destructive, and wholly negative or hostile to what they learned in their church or other religious education setting.

I can certainly understand their conclusions, but they are most often mistaken. Certainly a given professor could set out to destroy someone's faith, but most of my colleagues have deep faith lives themselves and profoundly respect the faith lives of their students. In addition, many Christian denominations, as well as Jewish traditions, value the critical methods because of the ways they support serious consideration and understanding of various theological issues. I include in this primer a brief discussion of some of these theological issues.

Sometimes people claim that to be a "Christian" means that you must believe that everything the Bible says is true. A related question and also a source of division for some Christian denominations is, who wrote the Bible? The question of how to read the Bible stems in part from this question of authorship.

When the word *author* is used today, it usually means quite simply a person who wrote the words in a text. While most Christians would say that the biblical texts were written by human beings inspired by God, the model for this interaction between humanity and God can differ significantly. Some Christians hold to a model of divine dictation: God telling a human author exactly what to write. Others think of inspiration differently, seeing the Bible as the product of true human authorship, while understanding inspiration to mean that God is encountered in an inspired text, not because the text was produced in some miraculous, otherworldly way, but because God chooses to be revealed in this humanly produced writing. Each religious tradition merits its own careful study to understand its view of human-divine authorship or inspiration, as well as the relationship of those views to the tradition's understanding of creation, natural reason, and other matters.

Furthermore, Christian churches also say that the Bible is *inerrant*, which means that it is free from error. While some Christians, such as many evangelical Christians, would say that everything in the Bible is inerrant, including scientific and historical information, others state that the Bible is inerrant in matters of salvation. What this means is that when the Bible communicates things that people need to know to live a life that leads to salvation, they can count on the Bible being free of error. This view of inerrancy does not depend on whether the scientific or historical information in the Bible is factually correct.

This primer is written from the belief that human authors acted as human authors when creating the biblical text. As such it assumes that biblical scholars must use every means available to understand that text within its own historical-cultural context, as a literary product, and as preached to living communities. This means that a biblical text can and should be analyzed in the same way as any other text. Students can ask about the purpose of the text's production. They can research the writing conventions at the time and look for other writings that may have influenced a particular author. They can uncover some of the unconscious influences on a work, such as assumptions about the relationships between men and women, rich and poor, Jew and Gentile. They can ask how the genre of the text affects its meaning. These questions and others like them help religious communities better understand the theological significance of the text, because they aid in the process of making the text understandable to a contemporary audience.

# PART 1

# THE WORLD BEHIND
# THE TEXT

This section is devoted to historical critical methods, that is, methods of biblical interpretation designed to place the text within its historical, social, and cultural contexts. Sometimes people refer to the historical critical method as if it is a single thing, which is misleading. Although these methods are unified in their aim, they represent a variety of different tools that aid in achieving that goal. For example, some focus on what we can know about the author of a given text, whereas others look at ancient cultural practices that explain the content of the text.

Although theologians have always been interested in the text's original meaning, they began to articulate the historical critical methods after the Enlightenment for many complex reasons, including the desire to settle disagreements and to provide more reliable ways to talk about the meaning of the Bible. To achieve these goals, they developed some standard approaches to interpretation of the biblical text.

Recently a scattering of critiques of the historical critical methods have surfaced. Some of these come from Christian theologians who conclude that the historical critical methods are either hostile to a theological reading or at least a roadblock to one. One reason this critique arose was that in its early days, historical criticism claimed too much certainty in its ability to uncover *the* meaning of a text. However, since at least the 1970s, biblical scholars have abandoned the claim that a text has only one given meaning that historical criticism can uncover. The kind of openness to meaning that some readers find necessary for a theological reading is no longer undercut by contemporary uses of historical critical methods.

In addition, most contemporary Jewish and Christian communities affirm the importance of the text's original meaning as a necessary element in considering its ongoing relationship to their faith community. The Roman Catholic document "The Interpretation of the Bible in the Church" (1993), for instance, states, "The historical-critical method is the indispensable method for the scientific study of the meaning of ancient texts" (sec. I.A.). Similarly, the *United Methodist Member's Handbook* states that the first question a reader of the Bible should ask is, "What did this passage mean to its original hearers?" This section of the book will first consider the following topics:

- the reconstruction of written sources an ancient author may have used to compose a text (source criticism)
- the oral traditions used by a given author (form criticism)
- the identification of traditions that an author employs in constructing new texts (tradition criticism)
- the way a final author has put a text together (redaction criticism)
- the historical circumstances that have led an author to write a given text (historical analysis)
- the role social location and social convention play in the way texts are produced and preserved (sociological analysis)

These methods help explain aspects of a text's production. They do not address every aspect of a text's meaning, nor its ongoing significance to communities of readers. These will be covered in subsequent sections of the book. From the start, then, it should be apparent that no single method of biblical interpretation is meant to stand on its own. Each is only one piece, or one set of questions, meant to break open the possible meanings of a particular text.

## SOURCE CRITICISM

Historical critical methods ask the researcher to imagine the person who actually wrote a particular text centuries ago. How scholars conceive of this person affects how they will investigate the history of the text's production. If a particular scholar holds a view of inspiration that imagines the biblical author simply copying down what he (and usually people assume the writer must be male because all of the scribes named in the Bible are male) has heard God say, then such a moment is unavailable to historical "proof." But if a scholar imagines someone passing on sacred lore, or recording an eyewitness account of events, or even inventing texts entirely, then the scholar might ask questions about where the author got this information and what things might have influenced the writing.

Historical research in any field presumes that human nature has remained relatively constant throughout human history. If readers take seriously the notion that God uses human authors as vehicles for divine revelation, then they should be imagining someone like us in an ancient context. For example, I would assume that if the author is trying to relate the history of Israel, he would have tried to produce one that conformed to the ancients' standards of historical writing. From what we know about history writing in the ancient world, while it would have included some use of sources to provide an accurate account of events, the author also would have enjoyed more liberty than a modern historian to manipulate those sources to communicate more clearly why he was telling this history.

In a culture where honoring one's elders was a vital social value, one which preserved oral traditions, I would also expect that the author would have had respect for the information he had inherited. In a society where the production of texts was expensive, I would also expect that any written sources he had available to him would have carried a certain weight, since only the most important information or traditions would have been committed to writing. Therefore, if an author had access to written material, he would likely have given that material serious consideration when he wrote his own text. Plenty of evidence from the ancient world suggests that this was the case.

In sum, source criticism looks for evidence that an author has used written sources in the production of a new text. It does this by looking at repetitions, changes in style, variations in vocabulary, and other such evidence that would result from an author combining previously written sources to create a new text.

## Old Testament

Source criticism arose from the evidence of the text itself and not from the recovery of ancient manuscripts. For example, scholars noticed that a text like Genesis, chapters 12–22, which in most respects seemed to be a continuous narrative, was in fact better described as a cycle of Abrahamic traditions that are episodic and disjointed. Some rather glaring anomalies in Genesis, for example, made this apparent:

- In three stories, one of the patriarchs claims that his wife is his sister, placing her sexual purity at risk. These three stories share many odd details that would not be the result of the retelling of a common story.
- In the story of the banishment of Hagar and Ishmael (Gen 21:15 – 16), the boy appears to be an infant or toddler. However, according to the chronology of the text, he is well over fourteen years old.
- In Genesis 6:3, God limits human life to 120 years, but Abraham lives to 175 (Gen 25:17) and Sarah to 127 (Gen 23:1).

Source criticism also provides a model for imagining the writing process that led to the Pentateuch (the first five books of the Bible) and other biblical books as we now have them. Using source criticism, scholars have developed models for understanding the anomalies and discrepancies within Genesis.

One of the better scholarly theories imagines the author of the Pentateuch relying on multiple sources when compiling the books. Archaeological discoveries have provided evidence that it was common practice for authors to freely use and adapt earlier material. It was a way of showing respect for earlier scribes.

By the end of the nineteenth century, a four-source theory for the Pentateuch was well established. Julius Wellhausen published the most influential version of this model in *Prolegomena to the History of Ancient Israel*, using theories of religious development in addition to literary cues in the texts themselves. Here are some of the features of each of the four written sources used by the final author of the Pentateuch as described by Wellhausen:

| | Yahwist (J) | Elohist (E) | Deuteronomist (D) | Priestly Writer (P) |
|---|---|---|---|---|
| **Date** | United monarchy | Divided monarchy | Reign of Josiah (Judah alone) | End of the Exile |
| **Place** | Southern Kingdom | Northern Kingdom | Northern Kingdom | Judah |
| **Divine Name** | Uses Yahweh throughout the Pentateuch | Elohim used exclusively until the divine name is introduced in Exodus | Not applicable | Elohim used exclusively until the divine name is introduced in Exodus |
| **Religious Features** | Sacrifices are offered in different locations; priests and heads of household offered sacrifices | Sacrifices are offered in different locations; priests and heads of household offered sacrifices | Only the Levites can make sacrifices in the one place God chooses | Only the offspring of Aaron can make sacrifices; a single place of sacrifice is presumed |
| **Literary Features** | Lively narrative and anthropomorphic view of God | Lively narrative and anthropomorphic view of God | Sermonic, with characteristic phrases | Preserves traditions, such as genealogies, precise locations, ages, and so on; regal view of God |

Currently aspects of Wellhausen's four-source model are debated, not because biblical scholars reject the idea that ancient authors used sources, but because they question whether four sources is overly simplistic. In addition, they wonder about the date and provenance of the sources.

Over the past century, scholarly convictions regarding the presence and identity of D and P have remained firm. These sources use distinct language and have a recognizable literary style. Each has a consistent theology. They probably represent the work of schools of thought rather than the production of a single literary genius because each source evidences the use and development of earlier material.

One of the big questions for D is its extent and date. Is D limited to the book of Deuteronomy, or can it be found in other parts of the Pentateuch? Did D redact the whole Pentateuch? What is the relationship between D and the history that follows in Joshua, Judges, Samuel, and Kings? Did D undergo major revisions, and, if so, which stage of the tradition's development is most important for understanding its purpose and theology?

The date of P is also a major issue for source critics. Is it the presentation of an ideal Israel from the Restoration period, or the laws of the priests of the monarchy? Is P the redactor of the Pentateuch or simply another source used by the final redactor? Is the presence of distinct material, like the Holiness Code in Leviticus 17–26, evidence of its sources, or does it show secondary additions to P's original work?

The material outside of D and P, which Wellhausen identified as JE, does not show the same cohesion. Can this material be neatly divided up into two separate sources (J and E), or does it represent a much more complex accretion of various traditions over time? Was this material the early base that influenced D and P, or was it a series of late traditions added to a D and P base?

These questions are too complex to address here, but they do reiterate that source critics are trying to come up with the best model to understand the production of a complex text like the Pentateuch.

## New Testament

New Testament scholars do not talk as much about source criticism as they do about the "synoptic problem." The synoptic problem means that three of the Gospels — Matthew, Mark, and Luke — have a significant amount of overlapping material. This overlapping material would not be expected if these were simply three separate eyewitness accounts of the same events. If that were the case, there would be considerable variety in the wording and style of these accounts. Instead, the material that is common to all three Gospels has a striking similarity in exact wording and phraseology.

This overlap has long been recognized by Christian scholars. Augustine tried to reconstruct the interdependence of the Gospels as early as the fifth century. However, in the late eighteenth and early nineteenth centuries, the most influential models for understanding the relationships among the three Gospels developed primarily among European scholars.

These models recognize that the three Gospels share some material, like the parable of the mustard seed found in Mark 4:30 – 32, Matthew 13:31 – 32, and Luke 13:18 – 19. In addition, Matthew and Luke share material not found in Mark, such as the genealogy of Jesus (Matt 1:1 – 17, Luke 3:23 – 38) and the Beatitudes (Matt 5:3 – 12, Luke 6:20 – 26). Most scholars believe that the authors of Matthew and Luke used Mark as a source when they wrote their Gospels. In addition, scholars maintain that Matthew and Luke had some other source in common that had not been available to or used by the author of Mark, which would explain the material they share that is not found in Mark. This reconstructed source is called Q, from the German word *Quelle*, which means "source."

The relationship between the sources can be illustrated with a diagram.

*Two-Source Hypothesis*

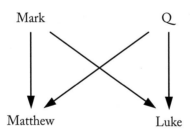

Today most scholars posit this relationship among the sources, although a significant number conclude that Matthew was the original source, used by Mark to a lesser extent and Luke to a greater extent. No matter what the specific reconstruction, however, the source method tries to explain the verbal similarity in different biblical texts by imagining an author using written sources to create a new work.

While the synoptic nature of the first three Gospels provides an important illustration of New Testament source criticism, the method is applied to other New Testament texts as well. Ancient languages had no quotation marks to signal material taken directly from other sources, but New Testament writers often used other conventions when quoting from earlier texts. Citing texts found in the Old Testament or in other works or traditions, for example, New Testament writers might use phrases such as "as it is written" or "now concerning" to alert the reader that the author is referring to another work or tradition. When these phrases introduce material not found in the Old Testament, scholars assume that the New Testament author is citing other written sources.

Changes in literary style are another important clue that a given author is using earlier material. Perhaps the easiest places to recognize these style changes are in some of the epistles that apparently quote parts of hymns (e.g., 1 Col 15:3 – 5 or Phil 2:6 – 11). Similarly, in a section of the Acts of the Apostles the narrator changes from an individual to a collective "we" (e.g., 16:10 – 17, 20:5 – 15, 21:1 – 18, 28:1 – 16). Scholars conjecture that the author of Acts has used an earlier source in constructing this history of the ancient church.

## Questions Source Critical Analysis Asks

1. Do repetitions occur either within one particular text or between one text and another that suggest an author has used a written source?

2. Could inconsistencies in the overall text be explained by imagining an author using a text that he does not alter, but that may have had an originally different use or purpose?

3. Are there significant stylistic incongruities, including the use of different names or technical terms for the same entity or the appearance of a different genre?

4. Can the repetitions and inconsistencies be grouped or reorganized to create two or more different texts that would be internally consistent?

5. If the repetitions are found in another ancient or biblical text, is it possible to argue that one was earlier and used by a later author?

## Exercises

1. Try to determine the source of a few passages in Genesis. Start with the examples of problematic passages already mentioned or with the story of Noah and the flood. Color-code each paragraph based on the divine name that it uses. Then read the paragraphs of like color in order. Think about what this method of biblical interpretation is best used for. What questions about the text does it answer? What questions remain?

2. Read 2 Peter 2 and Jude 3 – 16. What Old Testament references are the same in both passages? What is different about these lists? How would you go about determining which version is older?

# FORM CRITICISM

Another prominent method used in biblical interpretation is form criticism, which helps scholars reconstruct the oral setting of much of the biblical material. It is a complex method, so this guide will highlight only some of its main points. Form criticism originally arose in recognition that the ancient world was primarily an oral culture. In fact, form criticism was developed by Hermann Gunkel, who was influenced by a number of folklore studies that arose in the early twentieth century, including the work of the Grimm brothers. My description of form criticism tries to stick close to its original intention.

A form or formula is a phrase that tells an audience how to read or hear what follows. Originally part of the oral stage of material, forms are also found in written texts. A contemporary example would be the phrase, "Once upon a time." These words indicate that what follows is a fairy tale. It would be technically improper to use this phrase to introduce a newscast or a history textbook.

A form can also tell the audience something about the social location of the speaker. Today a minister starts a speech with the words, "Dearly beloved, we are gathered here today. . . ." In ancient Israel, prophets said, "Thus says the Lord. . . ." People outside a particular social location can use these forms, but when they do, they either take on another role or use the forms derivatively. Form criticism's recovery of a tradition's social setting is called the *Sitz im Leben*, or "setting in life."

Every society is filled with "forms," although not all forms are words. The modern phenomenon of channel surfing reveals the visual and verbal forms of various television programs. The screen for a home shopping network looks quite different from that of a crime drama. Even within a genre, such as music videos, distinct forms differentiate a country music channel from a rock video station.

When we study the Bible, we can only recover the verbal forms. We can't see if a prophet looked different from a priest, or hear the music of an ancient psalm. We can, however, detect patterns in the words. These patterns are forms. The patterns tell us what kind of material we have.

Today form criticism has developed beyond the initial phase of looking for oral forms and now incorporates other forms as part of its analysis. In addition, the search for a text's form has contributed to contemporary literary studies that focus on genre, while the search for a text's sociological setting has become a distinct biblical method. These will be discussed more fully as separate methods of biblical interpretation.

## Old Testament

In the Old Testament, one rich place to look for forms is in the prophets. Prophecy was primarily an oral performance, meaning that the oracles were usually spoken in some public setting. We see Amos, for example, delivering his oracles in the courtyards of the temple of Bethel (Am 7:10 – 13), and Micaiah ben Imlah among prophets gathered before the kings of Israel and Judah at a large public threshing floor (1 Kgs 22:10). Because prophecy was a type of oral, public performance, oral forms have been preserved as part of many of the prophetic oracles.

Scholars have recognized some typical phrases that open some oracles; these phrases are called *prophetic forms*. Here are the most common prophetic forms:

**Messenger formula.** A messenger formula begins with the phrase, "Thus says the Lord." It comes from the way royal messengers communicated in ancient times. A king who wanted to send a letter to another king sent a messenger, who would read the letter to the other king. The messenger would begin by saying, "Thus says the king," and then would read the letter in the first person as the king had written it. So when a prophet says, "Thus says the Lord," what follows is usually a direct speech by God that the prophet is announcing. This is by far the most common type of prophetic form, and it shows that the primary job of the prophet is to be God's messenger. Sometimes these oracles end with another stock phrase, ". . . says the Lord."

**Vision report.** Sometimes prophets have visions of things that represent an oracle. A vision report describes what the prophet sees and what the vision symbolizes. For instance, Amos has a vision of a basket of fruit. In Hebrew, the word for *fruit* is spelled the same way as the word for *end*. So the "fruit" means the "end" is coming (Am 8:1 – 3).

**Symbolic act.** Sometimes a prophet acts out something that symbolizes an oracle. For example, in Jeremiah 27 the prophet walks around Jerusalem with a yoke on his back. This symbolizes that the people are going to be "yoked" when they are conquered by the Babylonians.

**Woe oracle.** This is a little more difficult to recognize because translators render this differently. In Hebrew, this oracle begins with a particle pronounced, "Oy!" Sometimes this is translated as "woe," "alas," or "ah." These are always followed by an oracle of doom.

**Call narrative.** Many prophetic books have a chapter that describes how the prophet was commissioned as a prophet. Since prophets are God's messengers, they are "called" into service by God. The call narrative describes this event.

**Oracles against foreign nations.** Many prophetic books also have a section where some of the oracles that a prophet spoke against nations other than Israel or Judah are gathered together. Some prophets spoke oracles against Babylon, others against Assyria, and so on. These oracles, when collected within a prophetic book, are called oracles against foreign nations.

Prophets could also use forms from other settings to make a point. For example, in Ezekiel 19, the prophet sings a funeral song for the princes of Judah who are still alive. This would be similar to printing the obituary of your enemy, even though that person has not died.

## New Testament

Some Old Testament forms continued into the New Testament period, but they were joined to other new oral forms that developed in the Greco-Roman world. The Gospels, which center on Jesus' public ministry, preserve many of the oral forms used by teachers and leaders like Jesus. These forms include things like sayings, proverbs, and legal discourses. In addition, there are narrative forms, that is, stock ways of relating different events. A common form found in the Gospels is the healing story, which often includes among its stock elements the reaction of the healed person to the healing action.

One well-known Gospel form is the parable. Parables are concise stories that illustrate a single point using a metaphor or an allegory drawn from common experience. This point, which is not always obvious, is revealed at the end of the parable in a kind of "punch line." Like any complex metaphor, these parables often work on many levels. The parable of Lazarus and the rich man in Luke 16:19–31 is a case in point. The story uses a scene that would have been familiar to its audience (a rich man ignoring the plight of a destitute man even though he sees him every day) to illustrate not only the early Christian community's view of wealth and sharing but also to talk about disbelief and doubt.

Another prominent form found in the New Testament is the letter, or epistle. Letters in the Greco-Roman world had a set form, not unlike letters today. This form generally had distinct parts, including an opening greeting that identified the sender and the addressee, a prayer of thanksgiving or intercession, the body of the letter, an ethical exhortation, and a closing that could include a doxology. Most of Paul's epistles include these five sections.

Form critical analysis of New Testament texts helps a contemporary reader understand the distinctive elements of a given text. In addition, changes to the expected order can alert the reader to a point that the author is trying to make.

## Questions Form Critical Analysis Asks

1. Are stock phrases, patterns, or outlines present? How do these stock elements relate to the genre of the material?

2. Was a particular group associated with that genre, or was that genre used in a particular setting?

## Exercises

1. Look through the book of Amos and find examples of the prophetic forms discussed in this section.
2. Find a healing story in each of the three synoptic Gospels. What elements do they all share?

## TRADITION CRITICISM

Source criticism looks for evidence of written sources used by the redactor, while form criticism explores the author's use of oral traditions. However, the process of composition did not simply consist of cutting and pasting written and oral sources together. Sometimes the text results from a complex development of various traditions.

Many biblical scholars view the giving of the Law at Sinai as an originally separate tradition from the story of the Exodus from Egypt. They note that while many biblical texts outside the Pentateuch make reference to one or the other event, only late biblical texts connect the two. Tradition criticism asks about the process by which separate traditions, such as the Exodus and the events at Sinai, came to be linked. Similarly, the Passion narrative as evidenced in all four Gospels developed out of oral and written traditions about the final days of Jesus.

An exercise with a more limited issue in tradition criticism may help illustrate this method. A look at the Passover laws in Exodus 12:13, Numbers 28:16 – 25, and Deuteronomy 16:1 – 8 reveals that the redactor of the Pentateuch probably found these laws in various written sources. However, the laws themselves supply evidence of a changing tradition regarding how to celebrate Passover. A tradition such as this can have written and oral elements, and the changes can result from both formal changes made by authors or leaders and gradual changes that took place over the years, in this particular case as the festival was celebrated. Tradition criticism considers these laws and proposes a model for how they developed over time. Where possible, it also looks at references to the Passover outside the Pentateuch to help date the individual laws.

Tradition criticism can be used to trace the history of a tradition behind a text, as well as to discover how a tradition develops in written texts.

## Old Testament

Most Christians know the details of Jesus' arrest, crucifixion, and Resurrection best because they are relived every year in Christian worship services during important religious holidays; in the same way, the Exodus was so central to the Israelites that later poets and prophets could refer to just one small part of the story and know that the audience would recall the whole span of events leading up to and following the Exodus. The Israelites may have known the Exodus accounts because they heard them on their high holy days. This was certainly true once Passover, the feast celebrating the Exodus, became a regular Israelite ritual. Liturgy was and remains an important way oral traditions are maintained.

The book of Exodus has elements common to ancient folklore and traditional retellings of important events. For example, it does not give specific names of pharaohs, the dates of their reigns, or even the exact location for the parting of the sea. Instead, it focuses on God's deliverance of the Israelites and how Moses and the Hebrews reacted to God's activity in their lives. The author uses mythic elements to heighten the importance of these events. These mythic elements include exaggeration (also called *hyperbole*) and symbolism. These literary devices remind the reader that these are cosmic events that changed the world.

The various versions of the Exodus preserved not only in the book of Exodus but throughout the Bible give evidence that the Exodus event was an important tradition in ancient Israel (as well as later in the ancient Church). The echoes of the Exodus used by various ancient authors are not usually found as the verbatim copying of written sources nor as the written account of an oral form. Instead these were traditions known to ancient authors in multiple forms and in such a way that the author could draw on these various traditions to create new texts.

## New Testament

A variety of traditions can be found in the New Testament, including things like the practice of baptism or the form of the earliest Eucharist. However, to continue from our Old Testament discussion, we can also explore the ways that New Testament authors used Old Testament traditions such as the Exodus.

The Gospel of Matthew, for example, begins with a story of the birth of Jesus. In this version of the birth, the author uses images and motifs found in the traditions attached to Moses. For example, an evil king threatens to kill all the male babies born at a particular time. Joseph worries about what to do for Jesus, which parallels Jewish interpretations of the Exodus found at this time that depict Moses' father also worrying. Jesus is saved from this threat in Egypt, even though the author uses an ironic twist by making Egypt the place of deliverance. The author even goes so far as to quote a biblical text (Hos 11:1) to make his use of the Exodus traditions more explicit. The birth of Jesus, then, marks the beginning of a new exodus that will lead to a new kingdom, this time, the kingdom of God. The author of this birth narrative seems to assume that his audience would recognize these echoes.

Presenting Jesus as a "new Moses" occurs in other parts of Matthew's Gospel as well. For example, the Sermon on the Mount echoes traditions associated with Moses, including a discourse on the Law and a series of blessings for those who are righteous. Clearly this author wanted his audience to view Jesus as being in continuity with the Exodus traditions. The use of earlier traditions is an important component to understanding major themes that a text would have had in its original context.

## Questions Tradition Critical Analysis Asks

1. Does the text contain references to material found in other parts of the Bible?

2. After finding other references to the same theme, idea, or narrative pattern, can you trace a development of these traditions over time? Can you use texts whose date is more certain to help date material whose date is debated?

3. How does the use of a particular tradition in a given text help illustrate the major themes or viewpoint of that text?

## Exercises

1. Look at the slave laws in Exodus 21:2 – 11, Leviticus 25:39 – 55, and Deuteronomy 15:12 – 18. Try to trace the development of these traditions. Are they simply reflections of different historical time periods, or do they show conscious reworking of earlier traditions by a later group?
2. Look at the accounts of the Transfiguration in Matthew 17:1 – 8, Mark 9:2 – 8, and Luke 9:28 – 36. Look up the accounts of the deaths of Moses and Elijah. What kinds of traditions are
the authors of the Gospels trying to access in the story of the Transfiguration?

# REDACTION CRITICISM

Source criticism seeks evidence of different written sources that were used in composing a text, form criticism looks for oral components, and tradition criticism examines the use of earlier traditions. These critical methods go "behind" the text to investigate the history of its production as a way to explain such things as style, vocabulary, and literary structure, as well as repetitions and contradictions.

Source, form, and tradition criticisms aim to identify each separate strand in a composite text like Exodus, chapters 14 and 15. Redaction criticism examines how and why these strands were put together. Redaction criticism often goes hand in hand with these other methods because together they are tools for examining the history of the text's production.

Redaction criticism is most compelling when we have at least some of the sources that the redactor used. This is the case for the first three Gospels in the New Testament (Matthew, Mark, and Luke), which exhibit interdependence; likewise, it is true for 1 and 2 Chronicles, which are dependent on several other biblical books. In these cases, biblical scholars can see the additions, deletions, or rearrangements of material done by the redactor. These changes can reveal the particular interests or emphases of an author.

These examples serve as a model when the earlier sources no longer exist. Such is the case for the Pentateuch. Clearly the redactor used different traditions. Source criticism isolates these sources; redaction criticism asks why they have been put together in this particular way. In this sense, redaction criticism highlights the literary artistry of the final author. One recent biblical scholar likened looking at a composite biblical text to viewing a collage. The viewer recognizes that individual pieces had a prior life and context, but the artistry of the text results from the way these disparate units were put together.

The same is true for the redactor of Exodus describing the crossing of the Red Sea. He used earlier versions of this event, but he was no mere copyist. He intertwined these sources so that elements of each play off against one another, highlighting some elements and pushing others into the background. Redaction criticism recognizes the sources because the artistry of the final text is the result of how these sources were used.

## Old Testament

Perhaps the best place to begin an exploration of redaction is in the books of Chronicles. The author of Chronicles clearly used the books of Samuel and Kings as written sources in his production of a history of the kingdom of Judah. When parallel accounts of an individual event are placed side by side, such as the account of David's census of Jerusalem in 2 Samuel 24 and 1 Chronicles 21, the verbatim use of earlier written sources is plainly evident. Most differences between the two texts are minor, perhaps stemming as much from an alternate form of the text of 2 Samuel 24 as it might from conscious rewording. Examples such as these inform biblical scholars' imaginations about the use of unrecoverable written sources in other texts.

Some of the changes that the Chronicler (author of Chronicles) makes prove to be ideological and programmatic. In other words, they stem from conscious reworking of these earlier materials. One example of this is the way in which the Chronicler does not retain most of the negative stories about David. He does not retell the account of his affair with Bathsheba, for instance, nor does he recount Michal's criticisms of David. Another example of programmatic change would be his introduction of Satan into the story of

David's census, a change that matches his more transcendent view of God than is generally found in Samuel and Kings.

Because scholars have access to some of the written sources that the Chronicler used, much of the research on the books of Chronicles has focused on redactional analyses. These studies have been able to demonstrate this author's unique interests in the Temple, kingship, and God's immediate punishment of sin.

## New Testament

Since we looked at how the authors of both Matthew and Luke used Mark as a source for writing their Gospel narratives, it is not surprising that much of the study of redaction in the New Testament has also focused on the final arrangements of this material in each of the three synoptic Gospels. In the section on source criticism we focused on tracing the interdependence of one Gospel on another, attempting to reconstruct the chronology of their production.

Redaction criticism looks at a different aspect of this same phenomenon, paying attention to the changes one author makes to earlier material. This investigation depends, in part, on correctly assessing the chronological order. If Matthew comes before Mark, for example, then it would be more proper to consider ways Mark has altered material in Matthew, rather than vice versa.

To understand this method, it is probably easier to begin with Luke, which most scholars agree postdates both Matthew and Mark. The complexity of redaction criticism is highlighted by a text like Luke 6:17 – 39. This passage has material similar to Matthew's Sermon on the Mount (Matthew 5 – 7), but with some significant differences. Jesus is on a plain when he delivers the Beatitudes, not on a mountain. This speech contains both blessings and curses, while Matthew's has only blessings. Luke and Matthew both have a discourse on the Law, but Luke places Jesus' discussion of the Lord's Prayer in a later chapter (11:1 – 4). These differences have led scholars to wonder whether the author of Luke has altered the material in Matthew to fit the overall schema of his account, or whether these are simply two different reflections of their common source, Q. If the latter, they theorize which is closest to the original material and which shows the greatest change. This example demonstrates that verbatim parallels denote a relationship between two texts, but it does not always settle what the direction of influence may have been.

## Questions Redaction Critical Analysis Asks

1. When available, compare earlier and later versions of the same text. How and why has the later version changed from the earlier version?

2. When earlier versions of the same material are no longer available, after analyzing the material for the presence of earlier sources and oral traditions, look at the final form of the text to determine why the redactor has put the material together in this particular way. How do the different parts of the text relate to one another? Is there an overall pattern that explains aspects of the text's final form?

## Exercises

1. Look at the three wife-sister stories in Genesis (12:10 – 20, 20:1 – 18, and 26:1 – 16). List the ways that the three versions are the same. Then note how the second and third versions differ from the first one. What issues do these changes address? Why has the redactor retained all three versions in the final book of Genesis?

2. Compare the accounts of Jesus' temptation in the wilderness found in Matthew 4:1 – 11 and Luke 4:1 – 13 with the presumably earlier version in Mark 1:12 – 13. What kinds of changes do the two later texts make to Mark's version? Why might they make those changes?

## HISTORICAL CRITICISM
## AND NEW HISTORICISM

The phrase *historical criticism* can be confusing. On the one hand, it refers to all methods focused on the ancient meaning and context of the text, including source criticism, redaction criticism, text criticism, and so on. On the other hand, it is sometimes used to refer to the effort to reconstruct the history of ancient Israel. In this more narrow sense, the text is used as evidence for an historical reconstruction.

Historians use all evidence available to them. This includes archaeological evidence, texts found outside of the Bible, music, art, and so on. Historians know that their reconstructions are imperfect, but their goal is to account for the widest variety of evidence through their reconstructions.

The use of biblical texts in historical reconstructions has always been a tricky matter. For some people, the Bible's sacred character makes it a de facto reliable source for Israelite history. For them, the account of the reign of Ahab, for instance, is a direct window into that history. For others, the fact that this material has an obvious point of view or ideology makes it worthless for deriving an accurate view of history. Sometimes people who assume the general reliability of the biblical text are called maximalists, while those who are skeptical about its historical value are called minimalists. Most historians of the biblical period fall between these two extremes.

One question that arises with reference to the biblical text is this: What are these texts evidence for? Given that they were written sometime in the ancient period, they do provide some evidence of the issues facing Israelites or the early Church in the period in which they were written. Scholars can ask themselves, why would people during the monarchy have wanted to preserve the traditions about the patriarchs, or what can we understand about the early Christian communities that preserved each of the four Gospels? The biblical texts provide evidence of ancient history; the question is, what aspects of that history are they evidence for?

The latest development in historical criticism is called New Historicism. New Historicism is a term used for approaches that are more consciously aware of the literary and ideological nature of textual evidence. Rather than searching for nonbiased sources, New Historicism notes that all evidence has an ideology. Even an annal that records events is the result of someone deciding which events warrant recording. The solution for historical reconstruction is to embrace and explore the ideology rather than try to neutralize it. New Historicism applies this approach to all historical evidence. Iconography (that is, ancient pictures found on monuments, seals, etc.) inscribes its ideology in its pictorial record. Architecture embodies spatial hierarchy. Art serves the interests of some patron. New Historicism asks whose interests are served by each piece of historical evidence.

New Historicism also focuses on the ideology of the historian. There is no neutral historical reconstruction. It is always undertaken to serve some purpose. Again New Historicism does not seek to neutralize the historian's bias; objectivity cannot be a goal because it does not exist. Instead New Historicists advocate making the purpose for the historical research explicit.

## Old Testament

Historians of ancient Israel use the biblical texts more as evidence for issues facing the community at the time they were written than they do as direct evidence of the contents of that history. In addition, if they can isolate earlier sources that a redactor used, they can also use these sources as evidence for issues in the period of their composition. This is why biblical scholars invest so much effort in debating the date of various biblical texts. The Deuteronomistic history (Joshua, Judges, 1 and 2 Samuel, and 1 and 2 Kings) tells us more about Israelites in the late monarchy and early Exile than it does about the historical David.

One of the most debated historical issues in Old Testament studies the past forty years has been the question of the origins of the nation of Israel. The Bible gives two accounts of the settlement of the land before the rise of the monarchy. One is in the book of Joshua, which depicts the settlement as the result of a series of quick decisive raids on Canaanite cities. The other is at the beginning of the book of Judges, which begins by listing city after city that was under Canaanite control; for Judges, the settlement of the land was a gradual process.

Archaeology has weighed in on this question. In the early twentieth century, archaeologists concentrated on recovering large buildings and looking for texts. In the latter part of the century, however, efforts turned to surveying areas that represented the daily life of ancient people. In addition, as technology has improved, the dating of older sites has had to be revised.

By the end of the twentieth century, it was clear that the physical evidence of new settlements in Israel offered a third reconstruction of the time period. On the one hand, there is no evidence in large Canaanite cities of widespread destruction at this time, especially in the cities mentioned in the book of Joshua. However, there were new settlements in the central highlands, an area inhospitable to large-scale agriculture. While this might be evidence of a new group entering the area that later became Israel, the material culture of these settlements was in continuity with Canaanite material culture. Without a biblical text, the natural conclusion would be that these were built by Canaanites looking to make new settlements for some reason.

This example raises the question of how much historians should use the biblical accounts to reconstruct historical events. Is it proper to interpret the new settlements through the lens of a biblical account of a group of slaves fleeing oppression in Egypt? Or is it better to critique the biblical account in light of physical evidence evaluated separately from the textual account? People on both sides of the debate have accused each other of undue bias, whether in favor of or in opposition to claims that the Bible is sacred.

While classic historians remain at an impasse, New Historicism asks bigger questions: Why does it matter whether the settlements in the highlands are Israelite? What is at stake in the debate? Whose interests are served in either answer? By asking these questions, it becomes clear that this is actually a debate about the "truth" of the Bible, where "truth" means "historical reliability."

## New Testament

A similar issue can be found in New Testament studies. While historians of the New Testament period research a variety of historical issues, one of the most controversial, albeit ongoing, conversations in New Testament studies is the quest for the historical Jesus. On the one hand, this quest is to be expected. People have always wanted to know more about who the person Jesus really was. Certainly the Gospel accounts only tell us selective things about him, and they assume that we understand things like information about the fishing industry or what crucifixion entailed.

But the quest for the historical Jesus goes beyond this, asking how much of the Gospel accounts of Jesus are historically reliable. Given some discrepancies between Gospel accounts as to some of the facts of Jesus' life, not everything in the texts can be taken as reliable. For example, the Last Supper either occurred on Passover (Matt 26:17, Mark 14:12, Luke 22:7) or the day before Passover (John 13:1); both dates can't be historically accurate.

We saw earlier that redaction criticism uncovers the ways later redactors changed or shaped their sources to better serve their literary purposes. An ancient source notes that Mark's division of Jesus' life into a ministry in Galilee, a journey, and his last days in Jerusalem is an artificial organization imposed on the material.

In searching for the historical Jesus, historians try to get behind these later traditions to find some elements of the Gospel accounts that can gain general approval as being historical. This is not new. Thomas Jefferson published a version of the Bible that not only harmonized the Gospel accounts but also only contained those things he thought were historical; for him this meant deleting all references to the miracles or anything else that sounded superstitious.

Today New Testament scholars use different criteria to determine if something is historically reliable. Passages that show some unique characteristics that cannot be explained by stock elements or other parallels are viewed as authentic. If there are multiple attestations to the same story, and if they fit best in the context of ancient Judea, then scholars are more likely to view them as historically reliable. For example, Jesus' cleansing of the Temple that occurs in all four Gospels (multiple attestation) or Jesus' baptism by John the

Baptist (an odd detail since it suggests Jesus needed to be purified or have his sins forgiven) are often viewed as stemming from the historical Jesus.

Historical research into the New Testament goes far beyond this quest for the historical Jesus, however. Scholars debate whether the accounts of Paul's life in the Acts of the Apostles are more reliable than references in his own letters. Archaeological digs have uncovered many details about life in and around Galilee at this time. Even reconstructions of the reality of crucifixion have revised our pictures of Jesus' death. These elements help modern readers better understand an individual text.

Lastly, New Testament historians often focus on reconstructing the communities that would have been the original audiences for the various New Testament texts. For example, exhortations to stay strong under persecution in something like 2 Peter 4:15 – 19 suggest a community undergoing many trials. The pleas in the letter of James to treat the poor well in chapter 2 imply a community that has some wealthy members. These reconstructions of the world behind the text are part of historical criticism.

## Questions Historical Critical Analysis Asks

1. What date was this text written? What issues may this community be trying to address when writing this text?

2. For narrative material, what is the setting of the account or story? How accurate is the text in depicting this time period?

3. What archaeological evidence is there for the historical context of the author or the setting of the text? How does that evidence either help explain the details of the text or contradict the text?

## Exercises

1. Look at the various accounts of the siege of Jerusalem by the Assyrians. These include biblical accounts (2 Kgs 18:13 — 19:37, 2 Chr 32:1 – 23, Isa 36:1 — 37:38) and the annals of Sennacherib, which can be found in *Ancient Near Eastern Texts*, vol. 1, edited by James Pritchard. How would you decide which of these accounts is more historically accurate?

2. Look at the references to Paul's conversion in Galatians 1:13 – 24 and Acts of the Apostles. What can you reconstruct from these accounts about Paul's conversion? Can you find any other traditions about his conversion experience? Can you find stories of other conversions in literature from the same time period? How do these affect how you evaluate the evidence?

## SOCIOLOGICAL ANALYSIS

A more recent addition to the methods of biblical interpretation has been the rise of sociological analysis. This method of biblical interpretation seeks to uncover how different sociological groups functioned and interacted in the ancient world. Sociological analysis can have three different aims. First, it can provide a social description of how different groups interacted. Second, it can seek to reconstruct a social history of how different social relationships changed. Finally, it can use social theory to reconstruct gaps in the record.

While biblical scholars use many different social theories, all of them employ some form of comparative analysis. That comparative analysis can be localized, meaning that the scholar looks for parallels in cultures closest in date and region to the biblical texts. Or it can be based on cultures, ancient or modern, with social structures resembling those of ancient Israel. For example, parallels with other preindustrial, agrarian-based cultures may provide models for analyzing social phenomena evident in the biblical text.

Some theories of social construction are based on economic factors. Marxist analysis, for example, focuses on the way the means of production affect social rank, interaction of social tiers, social flexibility, and so on. Other theories are based on political factors, for instance, the difference between a society based on a monarchy versus one based on tribal organization. Some theorists have attempted to use religion as the organizing feature, resulting in the examination of a monotheistic society versus a polytheistic one.

Sociological analysis has been criticized both for its speculative nature and for the excesses of those who reduce all phenomena to a single model. But these abuses of the method are not unique to sociological approaches. Sociological analysis asks a different set of questions than other methods, questions aimed at leading us to notice a broader range of elements in the text, and often the examination of localized or sociological parallels do explain elements in the biblical texts in convincing ways.

## Old Testament

The sociological method asks what general structures in Israelite society shaped the way different groups acted. Are some aspects typical of a particular group? How did social concepts, such as honor and shame, affect behavior? How did structures of power and prestige within a group play out? Were there actions that people within that society would have understood that seem bizarre or foreign to us today?

One of the areas that has benefited from the results of social analysis has been our understanding of the family. This analysis helps scholars understand not just stories about families but also metaphors using family terms, like that of *husband* and *wife*. If we presume that the ancient Israelites had the same view of marriage that moderns do, we may misinterpret a text like Ezekiel 16 that uses the marriage metaphor to describe Jerusalem's relationship to the covenant.

How would someone go about understanding what it meant to be either a husband or a wife in ancient Israel? This is, in part, a sociological question. To answer it, a researcher would first want to look at other biblical texts about spouses. Such research would show that issues regarding the honor or prestige associated with being a good husband determine how a wife's actions are evaluated. A husband's primary duty was paternalistic care of his wife, not love or affection. The husband was responsible for maintaining the hierarchical relationship on which society was based. A wife, then, was valued for her cooperation with her husband and for bringing him honor. The use of the marriage metaphor in Ezekiel 16 assumes these concerns about honor and subservience.

Sociological method would also look at husbands and wives in other societies, tracing whether the treatment of a "bad wife" in these Israelite metaphors reflected the larger cultural context. For example,

Mesopotamian archives include texts outlining the physical punishment of an adulterous wife. Some sociologists would also look at marriage in similarly organized cultures today, whether that similarity is based on economic structures, political organization, or some other integrating principle. This examination would demonstrate how marriage functions in rural-based economies, for example.

Such sociological analysis would explain why the prophets often used a marriage metaphor when talking about the relationship of the city to God. We can only understand how the metaphor functions if we understand the institution to which Jerusalem is being compared.

## New Testament

Sociological analysis has had a major effect on the research of New Testament material. Much of this research has focused on the sociology of the Greco-Roman period, rather than the use of contemporary comparative material. New Testament scholars have fleshed out everything from economic disparity in the Roman Empire, to ancient Mediterranean views of honor and shame, to Greco-Roman practices of table fellowship. One example from these can be used to illustrate sociological analysis.

Dining in the ancient world was a highly controlled activity that reflected and reinforced social hierarchies and group identity. Men were seated at a table in an order that visibly communicated the rank of each person at that table. A change in seat literally connoted a change in rank. In such a society, dinner parties, including wedding feasts, participated in this social function. A host of a party wanted to invite the right people and would scrupulously avoid insulting guests by incorrectly placing them at the table. Such a faux pas would be social suicide.

In Judea, table fellowship was further complicated by dietary restrictions. If a host invited an honored guest who observed the Jewish dietary laws, he would insult that guest if he served nonkosher foods. On the flip side, a guest who kept dietary laws risked offending his host if he refused to eat food set in front of him, even if that refusal stemmed from religious reasons.

With these elements in mind, readers of the New Testament can better appreciate the scandal Jesus caused onlookers in the accounts of his dining with sinners and "lowlife" (see Luke 5:29 – 30). In the Lukan passage, Jewish religious leaders criticize Jesus and his followers for eating with the wrong people, such as tax collectors and sinners. Tax collectors often were viewed as traitors to their community because they collected heavy taxes for the Roman government that kept Judeans impoverished. In addition, they were often characterized as dishonest, extorting more money than was owed to line their own pockets. "Sinners" would have been a general category that included people with impurities or who were in a state of defilement. Jesus' associations with these social groups depict him as a social rebel.

Similarly, parables that use dining and feasting images, like Matthew 22:1 – 14, also play on social expectations related to dining. The kingdom of God is regularly portrayed as a place where the status quo is upended. Those who enjoy honor and privilege in this world are replaced by the lowest members of society. In this parable, the privileged turn down God's "invitation" to the banquet; in other words, they had the same opportunity to enter the kingdom of God, but turned God down. The result is similar to that found in the passage from Luke (14:15 – 24): Jesus preached a kingdom that looks quite different from people's earthly experience. Examining the social symbolism of things like table fellowship helps readers better appreciate the New Testament texts.

## Questions Sociological Critical Analysis Asks

1. Does the text stem from the interests of some social group?
2. What can you learn about the interaction between this group and others by surveying cultures with similar social groups?
3. Are economic issues that affect social structure a factor in the text?
4. How does this information about the text's setting in life help place this text in relationship to other social groups present at the time?

## Exercises

1. Marriage among the elite classes in the ancient world was not based solely on love. Instead, marriages were often arranged by the parents of the bride and groom. Within marriage, women were legal dependents on their husband; a wife could not even make a vow to God unless it was sanctioned by her husband. In light of that information, read Ezekiel 16. How does the metaphor of Israel as God's wife reflect the social status of a wife?

2. Look up the word *table* in Luke's Gospel. What activities take place at tables? In what ways do the passages feature who is at the table?

# PART 2

# THE WORLD OF THE TEXT

The first part of this book examines methods used to uncover the history of a text's production, as well as those designed to read the text within its historical context. In one way, those methods try to reconstruct what the text meant to its original audience. I acknowledge that even within this historical context, texts could have more than one meaning (polyvalence) and that ambiguity and polyvalence were attributes of literature even in the ancient world. However, recreating the historical setting—the social and cultural parameters within which this literature functioned—is essential for correcting misunderstandings of elements of the text.

Early in the Enlightenment, historical criticism arose as a method that aimed to settle disputes about a text's meaning. It aspired to develop "scientific" methods that would be objective and repeatable so that scholars could reach consensus on a number of interpretive issues and, ideally, advance the field of biblical studies. These aims took their lead from the natural sciences and reflected the admirable goals of neutrality, objectivity, consensus, and repeatability.

The effort had only limited success because interpreting a text is not the same as conducting a scientific experiment. Texts are not objects waiting to yield their secrets. Biblical literature is art, and, as art, its power lies in the way its impact and meaning resist simple categorization.

As the study of literature developed in scholarly circles, the results of this movement began to be felt in biblical studies. From the beginning of the twentieth century, some biblical scholars were applying methods of interpretation found in the field of literary studies to biblical texts. For example, Hermann Gunkel applied theories found in folklore studies to the study of biblical traditions, leading to the development of form criticism.

At approximately the same time, scholars in the field of literature became less and less interested in a text's production as the source for a text's meaning. Instead, they increasingly focused on the ways texts can be appreciated and understood even by people who know nothing about their author or historical setting.

Scholars have used many different literary methods to unpack the way a text communicates with a reader. One helpful way to organize these methods is to think about the elements involved in textual communication. Textual communication involves at least three stages: (1) An *author* creates a (2) *text* that is (3) "read" by a *reader*. (Theorists use author-text-reader to describe a variety of phenomena, including artwork: the artist is the "author," and the art piece is the "text," which is "read" by the viewer. This theory, therefore, is not dependent upon reading; it is equally valid for a work that is heard or viewed.) This schema raises the question, where is meaning located? Is it with the author-creator, the work of art, or the audience? When I say, for example, "This text means . . . ," what kind of a claim am I making? Let me go through each of the three options and relate them to different literary theories.

If I believe that meaning is something that stems from an author, I would see it as something deposited in a text by the author. My reading would be an act of excavation in which I would uncover the meaning deposited by the author. Therefore, the author becomes a focal point of my research. What is the author's historical setting? Do I understand the author's psyche? What has the author said about the text? Notice that this approach presumes that there is one (or at least a limited number) of answers to the question, what does this text mean? Disagreements about the text's meaning are adjudicated by appeal to the author's intent, understood within its historical context.

Of course, texts can mean more than what the author intends. To use an example from popular music, "Let It Be," sung by many Christians in honor of Mary, the mother of Jesus, was actually Paul

McCartney's tribute to his own mother. Does that mean any other use of the song is somehow wrong? Of course not. Pieces are deemed "art" because of their ability to "speak" to a wide audience.

Some methods of literary analysis focus on the text alone. The analysis of the text proceeds without reference to the author or the author's historical setting. The text is viewed as an artifact whose elements communicate independently of its author's intentions. Narrative analysis, which examines literary techniques, and some forms of rhetorical criticism, which look at how the text persuades the reader, focus on the text itself. These theories view multiple interpretations as not only legitimate but also expected.

Other theorists have pointed out that texts mean nothing until they are read. Meaning is created by a reader in the act of reading. Methods of analysis that highlight the role of the reader, such as reader-response criticism, start with the reader's conclusions about the text's meaning, and then look back at the text to trace the source of that conclusion. This approach is not interested in determining whether a reader's interpretation is valid; if meaning is in the mind of the reader, then there are no external criteria to determine validity. Contextual approaches to the text, such as gender and ethnic analyses, are a type of reader-response approach to criticism. These will be examined in part 3 of this book.

When literary criticism first arose, scholars would choose one approach and stick to it to the exclusion of all others. Today people realize that the acts of reading and interpretation are too complex to divvy up so sharply. Literary analysis is best done by recognizing that reading is the result of the interplay of an author's intentions, the text's structure, and the reader's social location.

This part of the guidebook describes methods of interpretation that analyze the text itself as a literary artifact. These methods are not meant to be exhaustive, but they do represent the methods that have had the most impact on biblical studies.

- Before an exegete can interpret a text, he or she must establish the "best" version of the ancient text (textual criticism).
- Literary techniques, such as characterization, repetition, dialogue, and parallelism influence the text's meaning (narrative criticism).

- Texts persuade an audience to view material from a particular point of view (rhetorical criticism).
- The text can also be analyzed with an eye on the effect it has on the reader (reader-response criticism).
- Texts also reinforce political and social ideologies, even if that was not the intention of the author (ideological criticism).

The last two methods function as a bridge to the third part of the book, which focuses on the text's meaning within reading communities.

The goal of this part is to introduce a sampling of methods that focus on the final form of the text. Often these methods work best when they are used together and then joined to the historical analysis that results from the methods discussed in the first part of this book.

## TEXTUAL CRITICISM

Before we can talk about what a text means, we have to decide what the text is. That may sound simple, but when the text is a piece of ancient literature that has been as widely spread as the Bible, it is not so easy. There is no single ancient copy of the Bible. In fact, the oldest copy of the complete Hebrew Bible dates from the eleventh century. Archaeological discoveries of the past century, such as the Dead Sea Scrolls, have provided scholars with much earlier witnesses to many biblical texts, but these witnesses show that there was rarely a single version of a text in circulation.

This is not surprising considering that there were no printing presses in the ancient world. Texts were produced by hand. The scribes who copied the texts also interpreted them. They had the freedom to adapt the text if they felt it would make more sense to their audience or if they had variant traditions among which they had to decide. In addition, the production of scrolls was an expensive process; scribes would have used the opportunity to update texts or make emendations to provide a "better" text. Similarly, when texts were translated in the ancient world, the translators could adapt them to better address their own audience's language, theology, and culture.

Copying is also not an exact science, even when the scribe does not intend to change the text. Sometimes the scribe's eyes skip words and part of a passage is dropped out. This is called *haplography*; a good example can be found at the end of 1 Samuel 10, where the description of what the Ammonites had done to the tribes of Gad and Reuben was missing in the Hebrew version but found in the Greek copy of the text. A scroll of Samuel found among the Dead Sea Scrolls, however, has the original Hebrew that stands behind the Greek version. Many modern English translations have restored this bit of text. A copyist could also accidentally write the same thing twice (*dittography*), or confuse the spelling of a word (*haplology*), or use a different preposition that means something similar. Examples of all of these manuscript errors, and more, can be found in ancient biblical texts.

One of the first things that biblical scholars do when they confront a biblical text is to consider the different ancient witnesses to that text. This is called *textual criticism*. Text critics used to seek the "original form" of the text, but today they are more interested in uncovering the various witnesses to a pericope (section of the text). Sometimes they will conclude that one version is older than another, but this does not necessarily mean that the older version is more authoritative.

Obviously textual criticism depends on an ability to read various ancient languages. However, even the nonspecialist can take into account various English translations of the Bible. The translation of the Bible into contemporary languages became common with the Protestant Reformation. Luther and other reformers translated the Bible into German; Catholics translated the Bible into English, producing the Douay-Rheims version in 1609. Today's translations, such as the New Revised Standard Version (NRSV), the New English Bible (NEB), the New International Version (NIV), and the New American Bible (NAB) take into account the many manuscript discoveries of the past century, and sometimes the notes in a study Bible will indicate when ancient versions disagree significantly.

## Old Testament

Most of the Old Testament is written in Hebrew, although a few sections are written in Aramaic. The earliest fragments of these Hebrew texts include some of the Dead Sea Scrolls as early as the second century BCE. Notice that these are fragments and not copies of the whole Bible. At this point in history, scribes had not yet developed a way to indicate vowels in a text; they only wrote the consonants. This leads to some ambiguity over the precise meaning of some words. The system of indicating vowels in Hebrew was not invented until the early Middle Ages.

In addition to these early Hebrew witnesses, there are ancient translations of the Hebrew Bible into various ancient languages. The most significant of these are the translations into Greek, known as the Septuagint, and translations into Aramaic, called the Targums (or Targumim). There are also Old Latin versions, Syriac, Coptic, Ethiopic, and others. Jerome's updating of the old Latin versions, known as the Vulgate, is a bit later than these earlier texts and depends on both the Septuagint and the Hebrew versions. Therefore, the oldest witnesses to the ancient text remain the Dead Sea Scrolls, the Septuagint, and, to a lesser degree, because of their free translation technique, the Targums.

While text critical analyses are not always terribly exciting for the person interested in the text's message for a contemporary audience, they are essential both for a discussion of the history of the text's production and, within communities of faith, for establishing the wording of the canonical or sacred text. At various points of Christian history, this effort has been vital.

The belief that Isaiah 7:14 predicts the virgin birth of Jesus is one such case. In the context of the book of Isaiah, this passage is not about the woman at all. The woman and her child are merely a literary device to mark off time in the oracle. The assumption that this refers to Mary comes from a text critical problem. The Hebrew text identifies her as a "young woman." It is the Septuagint that translates the word as *virgin*. Matthew 1:23, reading with the Septuagint, states that this verse is "fulfilled" in Mary's conception of Jesus. Christians can debate what the author of Matthew 1:23 meant here, but that is a separate question from the meaning of the text in the book of Isaiah.

In the Middle Ages, Christians assumed that Isaiah 7:14 had one and only one meaning, and that all other claims to what it signified were wrong. They believed that this text was so obviously about Jesus that anyone who would deny this must be evil, clearly an argument against Jewish understandings of the text. The fact that the Hebrew text does not have the word *virgin* led some Christians to assert that Jews must have changed the original wording of the text, and that the original text was preserved in the Septuagint. The Jewish leaders, they posited, changed the Scriptures so that their own people would not convert to Christianity once they realized that Jesus was predicted in their own Scriptures. These conclusions are found in medieval Christian polemical writing denouncing the Jews. It was not until the discovery of the Dead Sea Scrolls that the question was finally settled: the original Hebrew text at Qumran, predating the birth of Jesus, has *young woman* and not *virgin*.

While text criticism often operates on the level of individual words and phrases, it also deals with questions of a book's final overall form or shape. This issue looms large with several Old Testament books, such as Daniel and Esther, where their Greek versions are significantly longer than their Hebrew versions, or with a book like Jeremiah, where sections of the book are arranged differently in the Hebrew and Greek traditions. For Old Testament books preserved in Greek, like the Wisdom of ben Sirach, modern translators must also consider the Hebrew fragments of the book found among the Dead Sea Scrolls.

## New Testament

Text criticism for the New Testament is similar to that of the Old Testament. Scholars try to determine the best and earliest exemplars of a given text. They also must deal with various ancient translations in addition to the original Greek text of the New Testament books. They must consider when copyists have accidentally dropped texts, repeated material, switched wording, copied a letter wrong, and so on.

The earliest fragment of the New Testament is a fragment from the Gospel of John dated to the first half of the second century. Unlike Hebrew manuscripts, hundreds of ancient versions of the

New Testament are available to scholars. In fact, the earliest copies of the complete Greek Bible, the Septuagint, date from the second century. Because they are in Greek, they preserve the New Testament in its original language.

For modern Bibles, most of the text-critical issues that affect translations relate to what to do with material not found in the earliest manuscript witnesses. For example, the story of the woman caught in adultery in John 7:53 — 8:11 is found in no New Testament manuscript until the fifth century, although the story itself was probably older. Similarly, the reference to Jesus sweating blood in the garden of Gethsemane in Luke 22:43 – 44 is absent in the earliest manuscripts. Some modern translations of the New Testament place brackets around passages such as these to alert readers that they may be secondary.

Although fewer New Testament books are preserved in different forms than Old Testament books, the text-critical problem of the overall form or shape of a book also holds for the New Testament. The Gospel of Mark has been preserved with four different endings. In the shortest ending, which is preserved in the earliest manuscript evidence, the women who come to the empty tomb leave in fear and say nothing about the Resurrection to "anyone." The three longer endings bring the Gospel more in line with the other synoptic Gospels, attesting to the community's knowledge of Jesus' Resurrection. The textual history of these endings is complex and debated, so many modern translations preserve all four in one way or another.

## Questions Textual Criticism Asks

1. When analyzing a particular text, what are the various readings of this text in all its ancient versions?

2. Can it be shown that one reading is a later translation of an earlier one? Are there other explanations for variations, like texts being dropped out or material being copied twice?

3. What is the difference in meaning in various texts? Do texts simply preserve traditions that developed differently over time in separate locations, rather than result from deliberate alterations of an earlier text?

## Exercises

1. Read Esther 14 in the NRSV and in the NAB. What are the differences between the two versions? How do the differences affect the meaning of the text? On what basis could a scholar decide that one version is older than the other?

2. Read Mark 16 in several versions of the Bible. What are the differences between the various versions? How do the differences affect the meaning of the text? On what basis could a scholar decide that one version is older than the others?

# NARRATIVE CRITICISM

Biblical texts are literary artifacts, and their literary quality can be understood better through the lens of different modes of literary analysis. The most common type of literary analysis used in biblical studies is narrative criticism. Narrative criticism examines all elements of a text, including its literary techniques, to determine how texts communicate their meaning.

Like the other methods that follow in this part, narrative criticism presumes that the text's final form is a coherent whole, no matter what its history of production. The method is not completely ahistorical, however. It often attempts to understand the narrative elements within their historical context. The importance of the final form is seen most clearly in how scholars deal with repetitions, gaps, or discrepancies in a text. A source critic might use these elements as evidence for the composite history of the text's production. A narrative critic would presume that these literary features are meaningful elements of the text's final form.

Narrative criticism looks at all elements of a text, including the characters, setting, plot, pace of the narrative, discourse, point of view, and rhetoric. One of the most prominent features is the focus on the *implied author* and the *implied audience*. Some explanation of these terms may be helpful.

In reading a book like Ruth, we can assume the existence of a real author who lived in a given time period. Historians can try to discover the identity of this author, but that identity only partly explains the literary text. The book of Ruth itself has a narrator, and this narrator seems to be omniscient, meaning this narrator knows things that the characters in the book would not have known. In some ways, then, the voice of the narrator may sound like the voice of the author. However, on closer examination, the narrator does not know things that surely the author knew. For example, why would Ruth have given up everything to accompany Naomi? And why didn't Naomi tell Ruth that they had a kinsman who might take care of them once they arrived in Bethlehem? Analyzing the text in this way, we can surmise that the narrator is a character within the narrative and not identical to the author. Nonetheless, the text's various elements can be further analyzed to recreate the author that the text implies.

Another feature of narrative criticism is projecting the implied audience of a work. Ruth is read today by a different set of readers than the author assumed. An author familiar with today's audience would explain things that we don't know, like why the nearer redeemer removed his sandal. The text assumes that the audience knows about threshing floors and the kinds of festivities that went on once the grain was harvested. In other words, it implies an audience closer to the agricultural realities found in the text's setting.

One common approach taken by narrative critics is to interpret the text from the perspective of the implied audience. That entails many steps, including filling in gaps in our knowledge of the ancient world. It also means examining literary features of the text within their ancient literary context.

## Old Testament

Narrative criticism has been used primarily on narrative texts. Stories like those found in Ruth, Esther, and Tobit beg for a narrative analysis. These analyses take seriously the details of a given text. They note, for example, who speaks and when. They pay attention to who is named in a passage and who remains anonymous. They uncover the way texts use "type" or stock scenes within the narratives and when they make allusions to other texts. Most important, they note the pace of a text, leading interpreters to linger over passages where the narrative itself slows down. It is impossible to cover all of the literary devices that narrative analysis observes. I offer only a few examples.

One of the interesting features in this analysis is the examination of the character of God in narrative texts. For example, in a story like the creation of Adam and Eve in Genesis 2 – 3, God acts like a character in the story. In fact, at times the narrator seems to be more omniscient than God. After the humans eat from the fruit, God does not know where the humans are, although the narrator has told us they are hiding because of shame over their nakedness. Narrative criticism reminds readers that even the text's overt statements about God are part of the limited worldview of the narrative itself. Most Christians would not believe that God per se would have known less than a human narrator, even if they would appreciate or understand the way the narrative characterizes God's dialogues with the humans in that scene.

Another literary device that has come to prominence is the use of stock vignettes found in ancient near eastern literature. For example, the narratives describing the birth of a hero often start with a barren woman who is virtuous. Narrative analysis views variations in these stock scenes as deliberate changes that enhance the text's literary effect.

In Old Testament research, narrative criticism maps things like repetition, omission, and the placement of words as adding to the meaning of a given text. For example, exegetes of the Old Testament have noted the prevalence of something called *chiasm* in the way Hebrew texts are organized. A chiasm is when the beginning and ending of a text mirror each other, followed by the second element in the text mirroring the second-to-the-last element of the text, and so on. For narrative criticism, this organization highlights what is in the middle. A narrative analysis of chiasm will outline a text to discover the middle element that then becomes the key to the text's meaning. The focus on chiasm is especially prominent in analyses of poetic texts.

## New Testament

Although early studies of the synoptic Gospels focused on reconstructing the historical relationship of these three accounts, more recent scholarship has used the literary features of the texts to highlight how each presents a distinctive literary portrait of the life and death of Jesus. Theologians call the study of these different views of who Jesus is, especially with respect to his human and divine natures, *Christology*.

For a long time, scholars viewed the unique features of Mark's Gospel, for example, as evidence that it was early and, perhaps, more historical. The relevant features include the brevity of the Gospel, its sense of immediacy, and the way the text characterizes the apostles as less than heroic (not the sort of portrayal one would expect if the author identified himself with those followers).

While these features may or may not be evidence of the book's date of composition, narrative critics have pointed out how these and other literary features of the book work together to present a narrative whole. The narrative setting of the book is one populated by demons, illness, and impending disaster. The characters are sometimes "flat" representatives of types, like the legalistic Pharisee and the dim-witted disciples. The plot rushes forward to an inevitable end that is predicted three times by Jesus himself. And throughout the book the narrative plays with images of knowledge and ignorance, including a Jesus who constantly tells people "not to tell" what they have seen or heard, even though they usually disobey this command.

Perhaps one of the most intriguing features of the book is its ending. We saw earlier that the ending of Mark presents a particular text-critical issue. Which version of the book is its "final form"? Narrative critics, although open to analyzing each version as a distinct exemplar of the book, often prefer the book's shortest ending as the original. On the one hand, this preference is a function of the manuscript evidence, but on the other, this shorter ending is more in consonance with the narrative features of the rest of the book.

The shorter ending of Mark can be interpreted in a variety of ways within its narrative context. Let me give one example. Rather than tying up the loose ends of Mark's worldview, where chaos functions as an imminent threat to the cosmos, the shorter ending lets the audience reside in that tension. Women, and not the male leaders appointed by Jesus in the Gospel, witness the empty tomb. They react to the empty tomb with fear, not joy, and they are the first to keep the messianic secret by not telling anyone what they have seen.

The text's implied audience obviously knows about the Resurrection of Jesus, so the ending of the book seems to function on a different, perhaps ironic level. With whom should the implied audience identify in this text? It seems pretty clear that they are meant to identify with the witless disciples and fearful women. The book's Christology, or view of Jesus, places Jesus in the context of an impending confrontation between the forces of chaos (the sea, demons, righteous suffering, etc.) and the triumph of God's kingdom. The book suggests that this context is unresolved and seems to call the audience to make a different choice than that of the followers of Jesus in the book.

This analysis, while not meant to be definitive, illustrates narrative criticism's focus on the final form of the text, its endeavor to interpret literary features as constitutive of the meaning of the text, and its attention to all of the details of the literary elements of the text.

## Questions Narrative Criticism Asks

1. What does the text imply about the identity of the author? What does it imply about the audience? What is the relationship between the narrator and the implied author?

2. Which elements of the text are particularly featured in the text: the characters, the dialogue, the setting, and so on?

3. What are the main elements of the plot? What is the pace of the story? Where does it speed up? Where does it slow down?

4. What literary devices are found in the text? Are chiasm, use of stock scenes, or other devices present?

## Exercises

1. Do a narrative analysis of the book of Jonah. Who are the implied author and the implied audience? How are both Jonah and God characterized? Notice where and how animals and plants are mentioned in the book; what is their function in the narrative?

2. Look at the characterization of Peter in each of the Gospels. How does each text portray his character? How do those characterizations differ? Can you relate those differences to the larger features of each of the Gospels?

## RHETORICAL CRITICISM

Rhetorical criticism is another method of biblical interpretation that means different things to different people. Some define it as a method that focuses on material meant to persuade the reader; it examines the techniques that the writer uses to do the persuading. Others view it as an examination of the literary style of the text itself, regardless of audience or intent. Rhetorical analysis looks at the way the text achieves its persuasive, artistic, or informational effect.

We have seen in our discussion of historical inquiry that every text has a point of view. Although some texts are written strictly to persuade, all texts involve at least a subtle form of persuasion. They reflect someone's point of view, even when the author tries to write from the point of view of another person. For our purposes, then, rhetorical criticism examines all of the ways that an author presents a viewpoint.

Rhetorical criticism pays particular attention to the specific wording and structure of a text. For example, it might ask how the introduction of a text affects the way a reader interprets what follows. It might examine the structure of an argument being made, tracing how the author leads the reader from one point to the next. Sometimes rhetorical criticism takes note of what the text leaves out. It can even look at things like characterization and other literary devices whose purpose is to elicit a particular response from the audience.

One of the basic questions rhetorical criticism addresses is how does the text lead the audience to a particular interpretation? For example, 2 Samuel and 1 Chronicles contain two distinct characterizations of David. In 2 Samuel, he is a sympathetic but fallible human being who makes egregious mistakes, whereas in 1 Chronicles, he is a pious, flawless king. Similarly, each of the Gospels has a distinct characterization of Jesus. In Matthew, for example, Jesus is often portrayed as a new Moses, whereas in Mark, he is more often a healer and miracle worker confronting forces of chaos. Rhetorical criticism examines the ways that texts achieve these different portraits.

## Old Testament

Prophetic writing is a natural place to use rhetorical criticism. Clearly these texts have a point of view, and they are overt in their attempt to change people's behavior. A rhetorical analysis of an oracle would examine the way the oracle is persuasive. Take, for example, the oracles against foreign nations in the book of Amos. The book opens in the northern kingdom of Israel with oracles against foreign nations. The author starts by condemning all the countries around Israel, one by one. You can just feel the crowd growing as he condemns the Phoenicians, insults the Philistines, and prophesies against the Edomites. Next he turns against those rotten people in Judah, who think they're the chosen ones just because they have the Davidic king and the Temple in Jerusalem. Then just as he has a whole audience thinking, "This man is a true prophet!" he turns the focus on the audience themselves. The oracle of condemnation against Israel that follows is more than twice as long as the oracles against other nations. This demonstrates the prophet's use of effective rhetorical devices.

In exilic prophetic texts, elements of the persuasive nature of oracles remain. Individual poetic oracles, such as Jeremiah 3:21 – 22 or Ezekiel 19:1 – 14, use the same kinds of prophetic speech patterns found in pre-exilic prophets. The confrontation between Jeremiah and Hananiah (Jeremiah 28) and the disputation of the proverb in Ezekiel 18 present moments of oral persuasion. In both of these texts, the prophets try to change the prevailing worldview of their audience.

One of the rhetorical features of a biblical text is the use of characterization. In the book of Jeremiah, for example, the person of Jeremiah becomes an important tool in the way the book affects its readers. Through Jeremiah's laments, where he talks about what a burden his prophetic function has become, the audience identifies him as a sympathetic character. This empathy for the *persona* of Jeremiah makes the audience more accepting of his oracles, even when they are shocking or disturbing, like his demand that Judah surrender to the Babylonians (27:12 – 22). This is just one more example of how rhetorical analysis uncovers the literary devices aimed at changing the behavior or thinking of its ideal audience.

## New Testament

Rhetorical criticism has been less influential in New Testament studies, although it can be used with any New Testament text. For example, a rhetorical analysis of the Gospels could look at the way a Gospel is constructed, what elements it includes in the life of Jesus, and which details are left out. These elements contribute to an overall point of view on the nature and significance of Jesus.

Perhaps the easiest place to examine a rhetorical analysis of a New Testament text would be with some of Paul's epistles, many of which use the literary device of the diatribe. A diatribe is an ancient form of argumentation where a speaker states the opposing opinion and then proceeds to negate it. This can be seen, for example, in various places in the letter to the Romans.

The epistles in general often have the clear purpose of persuading their audience. Galatians, for example, opens with Paul's surprise that the community he founded is now following "a different gospel" (Gal 1:6), meaning that they are listening to different views about Jesus. A careful reading of the opening of this letter reveals that Paul faces serious opposition. First, he curses anyone who would teach the Galatians something other than what he has told them (1:8 – 9). He next defends his own integrity (1:10). Finally, he asserts a divine source for what he has taught them: Jesus Christ himself (1:11 – 17). This opening is meant to persuade the audience of Paul's authority and reliability.

A short letter, like the letter to Philemon, demonstrates other aspects of Paul's rhetorical style. In this letter, Paul sends an appeal to a Christian group with respect to Philemon's slave, who has become a Christian. Although scholars debate what Paul is requesting, the letter's rhetoric, with its emphasis on love and its appeal to "do the right thing" without commanding it, suggests that the request would have been viewed as improper, difficult, or controversial unless handled in this delicate way.

Rhetorical criticism helps explain elements in the text that might be missed without consideration of the text as a form of communication between a particular author and a particular audience. In some ways, the method shares a focus on the implied audience with narrative criticism, but it does so to reveal how the text tries to persuade the reader to accept its point of view.

## Questions Rhetorical Criticism Asks

1. How does the text lead the audience to a particular interpretation?

2. Are words or themes repeated in the beginning and the ending of the text? Are other repetitions found throughout the text? Does the placement of any material seem odd? Why might the author have chosen to structure the text in this way?

3. What is left out? What information would you have expected to find, but is not there?

## Exercises

1. Read Jeremiah, chapters 37–44, and Ezekiel, chapters 3–5. What do the different characterizations of these men suggest regarding the overall purposes of each of their redactors, particularly with regard to portraying the role of the prophet and the nature of God when Jerusalem fell?

2. Read the first letter of John. What is the author arguing? What elements does the text use to persuade the audience of this point of view? What does the text mean by the word *love*? Who are the objects of that love, and who is excluded?

## READER-RESPONSE CRITICISM

Most of the methods of analysis in this part have focused on the way meaning is embedded in a text. Literary analysis, however, also notes that meaning is, in fact, an assertion of a reader. In other words, it is the product of a reader's attempt to understand a text.

Reader-response criticism focuses on this act of reading. Like narrative criticism, reader-response analysis is not interested in the text's production or in the author's intent. Unlike narrative criticism, it does not focus on the text as an artifact, but rather as the locus where meaning is produced. In other words, the meaning of the text is the result of a reader reading it.

Reader-response criticism maintains that there are different types of readers who belong to different reading communities. We will explore this concept more in part 3. Here it may be helpful to contrast what many students experience: the perceived disjunction between what they have always thought a biblical text means and what their academic teacher presents as the text's meaning.

Reader-response is one way to explore this difference. For instance, sometimes a pastor will give a homily on a biblical text that will relate the text to that particular congregation. This pastor probably is aware of the scholarly reconstructions of the text's original setting. He or she may know about the sources the author used or the forms that structure the story. He or she may even know other narrative analyses of the text that place it within its historical context. But on a given Sunday, it may be more important to acknowledge the effect that this text has on these particular readers.

Reader-response criticism is one way to avoid the trap where a single reading of the text silences all others. It notes that a text will have different effects on different audiences. It validates various meanings actualized or produced by various readers. In this way, it does not view the different meanings produced by scholars and by pastors, for example, as a problem to be solved, but as an expected result of the reading process.

One of the fears of reader-response criticism is that it has no way to judge one reading as "better" than another. If this is the case, then the text can mean anything. And, if it can mean anything, then it really means nothing at all. However, this fear is unfounded, since critics do evaluate the conclusions of various readers. The question that perhaps most validates reader-response criticism is, what in the text led to this interpretation? Reader-response criticism is evaluated by its ability to "actualize" or "re-enact" the text. Just like a movie based on a book is judged by its ability to re-present the book in a new form, so too interpretations of texts are based on their ability to re-present the text.

## Old Testament

Reader-response criticism looks at the experience of a text not as a composite whole to be analyzed, but as a dynamic process that results from the act of reading. Texts are analyzed by their narrative flow. Reader-response criticism focuses on the dynamic of reading, rather than on the interrelationship of various parts of the text.

A reader-response analysis of Genesis 1 – 3 would focus on the way the account of creation in chapters 1:1—2:3 affects the way the reader interprets the rest of Genesis 2 – 3. While a source critic would exploit the differences and repetitions in the text as evidence of the composite nature of the text, a reader-response critic would ask how the creation in seven days affects the reading of the story of Adam and Eve.

On the one hand, reader-response criticism may look like it is anti-intellectual or part of a fundamentalist movement. While some instances of the method may, in fact, come from fundamentalist critics, this method simply notes that however the text has come together, the reader is confronted with a particular text in a particular form and responds in a particular way to that text.

What differentiates a reader-response approach from fundamentalism even more clearly is its willingness to read "against the grain" of the biblical text. This means that sometimes the reader is confronted with material that is offensive or unbelievable. The reader is not expected to read the text as true. The response of the reader can be an explicit rejection of the text's point of view. By highlighting the reader's experience of the text, this method does not privilege one response as the "correct" one.

Scholars call this approach to the text one of resistance. To give an example, the curse on the woman in Genesis 3:16 states that as punishment for eating the fruit, husbands would "rule over" their wives. This statement means that men in the ancient world were the legal lords of their wives: they could negate their vows, demand marital relations at any time, and control all of the family resources. Many contemporary readers of the text resist this reading. Their response is that this is a dangerous model on which to base marriage.

## New Testament

Reader-response criticism in the New Testament is similar to that in the Old Testament. The method analyzes the way texts are presented to a reader, analyzing their modes of discourse. Biblical scholars note that all of these ancient texts were primarily heard, not read, since scrolls, and later books, were expensive. Reader-response criticism's focus on the dynamic nature of the text more easily accounts for these texts as oral performance or audible proclamation. When looking at a text like the Sermon on the Mount (Matt 5 – 7), reader-response criticism examines the flow of the speech and the rhetorical features of the spoken discourse.

As oral performance, the meaning of repetitions shifts. Hearing a prediction at the beginning of a discourse fulfilled at the end is no longer a problem to be analyzed, but rather an expected element of an orally delivered text. When Jesus predicts his own death in Mark 8:31, 9:31, and 10:32 – 24, the reader anticipates the ending of the Gospel and expects a connection between the features of the prediction and the narration of its fulfillment.

Gaps in the text are another literary feature to which readers respond. Sometimes they await the filling of narrative gaps; other times they must simply experience them as elements of a text that is porous or ambiguous. The reader of Mark's Gospel is never told why Peter so consistently acts as if he does not know who Jesus is. That gap is a deliberate part of the story.

The most relevant feature of reader-response criticism, though, is its avoidance of claims to have found *the* meaning of the text. It revels in the polyvalence or multiple meanings of texts, since this feature is one of the expected elements of literature. While this method places limits on a text's meaning, those limits come from the text itself, and not from some extraneous parameters for interpretation.

## Questions Reader-Response Criticism Asks

1. What in the text has led me to my interpretation?
2. What does the text expect of me as a reader? How do I experience this text as it moves forward?

3. What would a reading that either resists the text or reads "against the grain" of the text look like?

## Exercises

1. Read the book of Ruth in order. How does the text lead the reader through the story? Where does the text expect the reader to look back and rethink earlier parts of the book? Where does the text clarify earlier ambiguities in the text?

2. Look at the predictions of his death spoken by Jesus in the Gospel of Mark. How do those predictions affect the way the interim texts are read and interpreted? How does the ending of the book relate to those predictions?

# IDEOLOGICAL CRITICISM

Ideological criticism refers to methods of interpretation that try to uncover the unexpressed ideologies that lie behind the text. These approaches reveal ways that texts reinforce assumptions about social groups that can lead to inequities in power and status. Originally ideological criticism began as an outgrowth of class analysis using Marxist theories. Now it has expanded because of the recognition that other categories of human existence, such as gender and race, are also important features of social status. Some scholars use this designation for methods that deal with the ideologies of contemporary interpretations, such as feminist criticism, liberation criticism, and postcolonial criticism, which will be discussed in part 3. This is certainly one of its functions. Others use it as an historical method in its aim to uncover the ancient ideology behind a text. However, ideological criticism also aims to unmask the ideological bent of the text itself, even if this bent is not intended by the author. As a hybrid criticism whose three steps include the world behind the text, the text itself, and the world of the reader, I include it here.

Examples of ideological criticism abound in our contemporary culture. For instance, speakers on talk radio sometimes refer to the "feminist (or gay or liberal or conservative, and so on) agenda."

Popular pundits "unmask" the ways certain groups promote their agenda. In a sense, the pundits are doing ideological criticism. Notice its negative connotation, however. Pundits never accuse anyone of a hidden agenda if they agree with her or his position. In the popular media, ideology often has a similar negative connotation because most people like to think of themselves as ideologically independent.

The difference between modern claims that someone has an agenda and ideological criticism is that the latter does not assume that all ideologies are bad. In fact, biblical scholars who conduct ideological criticism would maintain that everyone has an ideology (an agenda, if you will) and that we only resist those with which we disagree.

Many ideologies can be invisible to those who hold them. Think about some commonly held beliefs. What principles do they assume as natural? For instance, the assumption that belief in one God is naturally superior to belief in many gods is so common that many people do not question that claim. Ideological criticism would seek to uncover why that assumption is so tightly held. For example, does anyone benefit from this belief in terms of prestige, money, or status? Could a polytheist accuse a Christian of having a monotheistic agenda? That question may seem silly, but it does illustrate the purpose of ideological criticism.

This approach to biblical texts assumes that at least one factor behind a text's composition serves some group's purpose or interest. This ideological purpose is usually masked, and it is therefore more influential because it is not overt. Ideological criticism tries to bring these motivating factors to light.

Sometimes a text's ideology is advanced by what it asserts. For instance, the elevation of the Zadokite priests in Ezekiel, or the elevation of the poor in the parable of Lazarus in Luke both present an overt ideology that elevates one social group over others. A text can also express an ideology by how it presents its opponents. In the same passage of Ezekiel 44, the Levites are depicted as those who let foreigners into the temple, while the rich man in Luke 16:19–31 presents a caricature of the opposing social group.

Ideological criticism looks at three elements of the text. First, it uncovers the text's production within its historical, ideologically charged context, seeking to uncover what issues the text addresses. Second, it analyzes the text to show where the hidden ideology makes itself evident. Third, the method looks at the text's use by various reading groups, each with a particular ideology that it is trying to advance.

## Old Testament

Ideological criticism looks at the three elements of the Old Testament text just mentioned. This can be illustrated by the polemics against idols in Isaiah 44:9 – 20. Ideological criticism first uncovers the text's production within its historical, ideologically charged context. Since this text dates to the end of the Babylonian exile and is written from the perspective of those in Babylon, it is not surprising that the text reflects the Babylonian practices of making statues of their gods. Here the passage ridicules this practice.

Second, ideological criticism analyzes the text to show where the hidden ideology makes itself evident. It might seem that the text's view of God's transcendence is based simply on theological or religious principles, but ideological criticism uncovers the political motivation behind the insistence on this view of God. Within this context, ideological criticism reveals that the Israelites were struggling to maintain their own identity in part because so many exiled Jews had begun to assimilate to Babylonian culture. This passage, which appears to ridicule the Babylonians, is actually directed against Jews who might want to imitate Babylonian religious practices.

Third, the method looks at the text's use by various reading groups, each with a particular ideology that it is trying to advance. For example, one biblical scholar from India, George Soares-Prabhu, has written about the mix of politics and religion in this text from the perspective of his own experience of religion in India. This last use of ideological criticism leads into the contextual criticisms to be studied in part 3.

## New Testament

Ideological criticism of the New Testament shares the same complexity as it does for the Old Testament. As the *Dictionary of Biblical Interpretation* states, "Ideological criticism investigates (1) the production of the text by a particular author in a specific, ideologically charged historical context, (2) the reproduction of ideology in the text itself, and (3) the consumption of the text by readers in different social locations who are themselves motivated and constrained by distinct ideologies" (p. 535).

Early uses of the method, influenced by Marxist analysis, focused on class issues. In New Testament studies, the harsh realities of the economic and social structures of the Roman Empire have greatly informed contemporary analyses of these issues in the New Testament texts. For example, several epistles focus on proper conduct for the new Christian communities. Although these rules for proper conduct sound like general statements that should hold for anybody, ideological criticism uncovers that they stem from various social and economic factors that affected this new religious movement. For example, the epistle of James focuses on the interactions of rich and poor within the community. This focus comes from the reality that the widespread level of poverty in the Roman Empire required people to join an association to pool resources and benefit from a rich patron or benefactor. These admonitions stem from the reality that the poor had no other place to turn. Similarly, the exhortations to avoid disgraceful conduct in 1 Peter derive as much from the group's need to avoid persecution as they do from general moral principles. Both analyses read the ideologies of the text within their historical context.

Even though these ideologies stem from an historical reality, the text also reproduces certain assumptions about social structure. Notice that neither James nor 1 Peter questions some of the elements of social hierarchy within which they function. They advocate neither an economic revolution nor an obliteration of social hierarchy by denouncing slavery, for example. They assume these divisions are "natural." The task of ideological criticism is to uncover these assumptions.

This method has also had an effect on the way certain images of poor people, women, and people with diseases have continued to affect Christian churches. Ideological criticism traces the use of these texts and others like them to keep women in a socially subordinate position or to avoid sweeping economic reform that would benefit the poor. Again this last aim of ideological criticism is best illustrated by the methods in part 3 of this book.

## Questions Ideological Criticism Asks

1. What issues does the text address? Who is the "ideal" audience presumed by the text? How are opposing viewpoints portrayed?
2. Where does the text's hidden ideology make itself evident?
3. Who benefits from the ideology of the text?

## Exercises

1. Ideological criticism can unveil the differences between contemporaneous prophets like Isaiah and Micah. Do they have different presuppositions about God and the nation? Do their differences stem from different social locations? Do their oracles advance the worldview of the group to which they belong? What groups today would prefer the message of Isaiah to that of Micah, and why? Who might prefer Micah, and why?
2. Look at the portrayal of women in the Gospel of Luke. How does Luke's portrayal reflect the social and economic circumstances of women in Judea during the Roman period?

# PART 3

# THE WORLD
# THE TEXT CREATES

How does the meaning that a text had in the past relate to the meaning that it has for reading communities today, especially when that community is a faith-based organization that embraces that text as sacred scripture? Should that religious group simply assume that what the text said in its original context remains binding for them today? More specifically, with regard to the Christian Scriptures, what about the law of the ban? or capital punishment for those caught in adultery? or polygamy? These examples demonstrate the difficulty of bridging the gap between what a text originally meant and what its significance or function is for a reading community today.

The theory concerning how one bridges that interpretation gap is called *hermeneutics*. Hermeneutics is a complex area, involving issues of meaning and interpretation. For our purposes, we will focus on this basic question: what is the relationship between what a text meant at the time it was composed and what it means for communities today? Hermeneutics surrounds us, even if we are unaware of it. Whenever you hear a claim that something is wrong because the Bible says so, that's a hermeneutical claim, the claim of a contemporary reader, from a particular perspective, regarding the meaning and application of a specific biblical text.

This issue is important for two reasons. First, a claim based on the Bible has a certain amount of authority for many people. This authority requires that we not treat such claims casually. Second, often when people make these claims, the assumptions underlying these statements are invisible, even to those making them.

Although hermeneutics has always been a significant part of biblical interpretation, from the 1960s onward, it has taken on new life as academic study of the Bible has become increasingly available to more diverse groups. The rise in the number of women and ethnic minorities in U.S. theological graduate schools, for example, has led to the awareness that some of what was formerly taken as objectively "true" in biblical scholarship was really the interpretation of a particular, dominant social class.

The approaches to interpretation that focus on hermeneutical issues are not methods of interpretation in the same sense as those in the previous two parts of this primer. Those methods focused on the aspects of a text's meaning that come from *outside* the interpreter. In other words, they aimed to isolate elements in either the text's production or in the text itself that shaped the overall meanings of the text.

The approaches in part 3 arise from the interpreter's social context, exploring how texts have either affected diverse communities or been read by those communities. Because these methods have arisen in the wake of postmodernism, part 3 includes an overview of this intellectual movement and the most prominent theoretical method coming from postmodernism, deconstructionism.

## READING COMMUNITIES

Part 3 focuses on the ways reading communities contribute to the evaluation of interpretations of biblical texts. By identifying "reading communities," scholars seek to move away from an overly individualistic reading of a text, as if individual readers are self-authorizing. Such early focus on the individual reader fed into the misconception that the validation of a text's possible meaning rests with an individual. Today literary critics understand that all interpretations take place within communities that both shape and validate those interpretations. Any reader is part of a reading tradition or community.

Reading communities cluster around any text. Shakespeare's plays have one reading community among scholars of Shakespeare and another among film producers of Shakespeare. In other words, their interpretations stem from a dialogue with others in that group who came before them or who work simultaneously with them. In addition, all individuals belong to more than one reading community. A scholar of Shakespeare may also produce a movie of one of his plays, for example. But reading communities also take into account a person's social class, gender, religion, ethnicity or nationality, and so on.

Because of the sacred nature of the biblical text, specific reading communities have formed around it, communities that often spell out specific guidelines for interpretation appropriate for this sacred text. The U.S. fundamentalist movement of the late nineteenth century, for example, grew out of concerns about the proper way to interpret the Bible. The Roman Catholic Church has issued a number of statements in the twentieth century about proper ways to interpret the Bible, with the latest statements contained in a 2008 document coming out of the Synod on the Word of God.

These communities of faith include diverse people: rich people and poor people, workers and owners, men and women, people from around the globe, physically challenged people and able-bodied people, and so on. In other words, churches and synagogues include people with multiple overlapping reading communities. A male CEO of a U.S. corporation may read a biblical text differently from an African woman infected with HIV and battling starvation, even if both are Catholic. Communities of faith have become increasingly aware that their guidelines for biblical interpretation have to be sufficiently broad to accommodate these varying perspectives.

Because some of the methods of interpretation discussed in this part challenge some of the long-held assumptions of what individual biblical texts mean, readers who are new to these approaches often mistakenly assume that some of these reading communities are hostile to faith or not theological. While certain individuals within each group may not be religious, most of these communities arose among people of faith who are trying to expand the theological meanings of texts to include diverse perspectives.

Because reading communities arise out of all kinds of social groupings, it is impossible to survey them all. I have chosen those that have had the most influence on the scholarly biblical community in the United States. For example, biblical scholars now regularly take into account gendered perspectives on biblical texts. But because one cannot "do" one of these readings without belonging to a particular community, I do not include discussions of how to do each method. Instead, I first describe the approaches common to all of these and then offer some representative examples. However, I do provide exercises designed to engage students with the approach or assumptions of each method.

## DIALOGUING WITH READING COMMUNITIES

The starting point for any of these methods is the recognition that no reader is a blank slate who contributes nothing to the meaning of a text. In fact, the claim that a text "means" something is a claim made by a reader, not a claim of the text or its author. Neither is someone who has never even heard of the Bible a better interpreter than someone who has lived with it, read it repeatedly, heard it in various settings, and so on.

Most people who study the Bible and make claims about its meanings come from explicit reading communities, a fact that sometimes has met with disfavor as it implies that any reading carries a group bias. Following the Enlightenment in the eighteenth and nineteenth centuries, the goal of biblical interpretation was to get past these communities to give a "neutral" or "objective" interpretation of the text. This goal was seen as important because it allows readers to get beyond hidden assumptions about the text that derive from their community's identity and perspective, and, theologically, it allows the text to have some autonomy to continue to shape communities of faith and serve as a guide for a religious community.

Although this movement toward more objective reading continues to be important for biblical interpretation, in the second half of the twentieth century, scholars began to recognize that the goal of objectivity did not exhaust the meaning of a text. Many factors led to this realization, but one of the most profound was the Holocaust. For many Christians, the reality that the Holocaust occurred in a Christian community that had deep Christian roots and that some Nazis defended their position through their interpretation of the Bible caused Christians worldwide to re-examine the importance of how certain biblical interpretations might be used. In other words, just because a particular reading can be supported by a biblical text does not make it the best reading for a modern faith community.

Scholars who interpret the Bible using the approaches discussed in this part usually begin by identifying their own reading community. Each of the following approaches can examine two aspects of the text: how the text's historical or textual meaning is understood from a particular perspective and the effect that various claims of meaning have had or still have on diverse communities. For example, an African American reading of the text may focus on the historical reconstruction of the practice of slavery found in the Bible. Or it may look at the way the biblical text was used to legitimate U.S. slavery in the nineteenth century.

People who are not African American need to consider these readings for two corresponding reasons. First, this approach involves the recovery of traditions that have been ignored by readers not affected by the same issues. These studies often point out things in the text that are important to notice. Second, this approach can help readers be more sensitive to interpretations that may inadvertently harm them and others.

Lastly, these approaches are not to be contrasted with some fictional "plain meaning" of the text. The ultimate goal of these approaches is to make us all aware that any interpretation is limited by our own experience, even those that have been considered plain and objective within our own traditions.

# POSTMODERNISM AND DECONSTRUCTIONISM

We live in the postmodern age, an age when claims for objective truth, certitude, and universal principles are met with skepticism. Some people say that this skepticism is part of the degeneration of our age; they long to return to an age of certainty. But the fact remains that a number of things have contributed to this methodological doubt.

As we have discovered, people now realize that much of what passed for universal truths were simply the conclusions of a select and homogeneous group of scholars, leaders, and authority figures.

Postmodernism refers to intellectual movements that recognize that all knowledge is constructed within specific cultural contexts. It highlights the subjective element involved in all claims of knowledge and truth. It also avoids evaluative statements. For example, postmodern art critics would not distinguish between "high" and "low" art; graffiti is as much art as is a classical oil painting.

One movement within postmodernism is deconstructionism. Both terms have a variety of meanings, but in our context deconstructionism refers to three primary approaches to biblical interpretation. First, deconstructionism seeks to uncover the ways in which interpretations that result in claims of objectivity and truth mask attempts to establish privilege for a particular group. For example, a claim that the Bible objectively calls for wives to obey their husbands is read by a deconstructionist as an attempt to maintain patriarchal authority by attaching it to a text viewed as sacred by those involved in the oppression.

Second, deconstructionism also seeks to uncover the ways the text masks the attempts of the people that produced it to maintain their own power. A deconstructionist analysis of the Deuteronomistic history would view the history as an attempt by a small group of Levites to assert their own ideology.

Third, deconstructionism also uncovers the ways that the dominant paradigm of the text, its central ideology, is often undercut by its own text. For example, the claim of the absolute authority of men over women in a prophetic metaphor such as Ezekiel 16 (the city as God's whoring wife) betrays male anxiety over their inability to control women's behavior.

For some biblical theologians, postmodernism and deconstructionism can pose a problem. In some forms, these approaches seem to reduce the biblical text to nothing more than political propaganda, the products of self-interest. However, in traditions that allow for the full range of human activity in the production of biblical texts, such human motivation does not limit God's ability to use the texts as vehicles of authentic revelation. The view that the texts are revelatory is a statement of faith in the activity of God; it is not an assertion about how the texts were produced.

Even if people today have never read deconstructionist theory, its influences are far reaching. For example, many biblical scholars now reject the notion that there is one or even a limited number of biblical themes or ideas. They point to the variety of voices in the text, and they stress that any attempt to reduce these voices diminishes the text we have received. These approaches to biblical interpretation have resulted in a much more accurate appreciation of the variety of texts in the Bible and, thus, in a more nuanced and accurate assessment of the Bible's contribution to theology.

In addition, these approaches match up better with many people's distrust of the claims of biblical authority often asserted in traditional theology. A postmodern approach views the questioning of such claims as a legitimate and essential element in thinking about the text's continued meaning for reading communities.

## Exercise

Texts that deal with the problem of discerning true versus false prophecy are really addressing questions of religious authority: Who do you believe? Why do you believe this person or group? Look at a text that centers on this issue, such as 1 Kings 22, Mark 8:27 – 30, Matthew 16:13 – 20, or Luke 9:18 – 22. How does the text address the issue of uncertainty? Would a contemporary audience faced with the question of legitimate religious authority address the issue in the same way?

# POSTMODERN APPROACHES TO BIBLICAL INTERPRETATION

## The Canonical Approach

The canonical approach describes a theological stance that a reader may take when approaching the biblical text. It is not a specific method of biblical interpretation, although its articulation has led to new movements in biblical inquiry. It is a movement within postmodernism because it takes seriously the theological context of Christian readers of the biblical text.

Canonical criticism has been used to label two separate but interrelated tasks. One task seeks to reconstruct the process by which biblical books came to have authoritative status. In this task, the focus is historical, but it traces the history of a given text beyond its mere production to the change in its status within various faith communities. This field has seen a number of important studies on a previously ignored aspect of the text's history.

More often, however, the canonical approach refers to those interpretations that read a particular biblical text within the context of the canon as a whole. This approach, started by Brevard Childs, originally sought to describe the way many "people in the pews" read the text. He noted that Christians, for example, usually do not read a book like Isaiah in isolation from New Testament uses of the text. He notes that if one is doing theological inquiry, then one should ask theological questions and use a method appropriate for that inquiry. For Childs, awareness of a text's placement within the larger canon is an essential element of most Christian theological endeavors.

Childs' approach to biblical theology has had wide influence, although different theologians use this approach in different ways. Three of the most prominent understandings of it are (1) the examination of conscious reuse of material; (2) the focus on the history of interpretation of a text within a given community of faith; and (3) the effect that canonical placement has on a reading community. Let's examine each of these in turn.

## Conscious Reuse of Material

Recent work on the Bible has looked at ways later authors and redactors make references and allusions to earlier texts. This conscious echoing, or rereading (in French, *relecture*), tells the audience that a given work is supposed to be read within a larger literary context. Biblical texts are not simply self-referential, but they tease out ideas present in earlier traditions. For some scholars, this tendency to connect originally isolated literary pieces can be seen in the final formation of the twelve minor prophets and the book of Psalms. An abundance of intertestamental allusions across the canons of the Old and the New Testaments affect the reading tradition. This awareness invites the interpreter to read the text within ever-widening literary contexts.

## Interpretation of the Text within a Faith Community

Although the formation of the final form of the text provides one guide to reading, for a community of faith, another guide is the interpretive tradition of which it is a part. Catholics read the Bible through the lens of influential theologians such as Thomas Aquinas. Lutherans are informed by Luther's own attitude toward biblical interpretation. In the nineteenth and twentieth centuries, biblical scholars needed to free themselves from traditional interpretations so that they could move forward in their appropriation of new methods of biblical interpretation. Now, however, there is a desire to recover some of that interpretive tradition. In some ways, this movement echoes the postmodernist approach that encourages readers to be aware of the interpretive context that informs their work. However, in the canonical approach, this focus aids the reading community's theological discussion of a given text. Canonical approaches can highlight the history of the interpretation of the text as part of this theological endeavor.

## Effect of Canonical Placement

Third, some canonical critics focus on the ahistorical or unintentional meaning created by putting disparate texts together. These scholars are not trying to make some sort of historical argument that a later author is consciously using earlier material, but they note that a book like Isaiah is read differently simply by being placed in a collection with New Testament texts. Scholars who examine these materials under the rubric of "canonicity" sometimes presume that the divine author intended the juxtaposition of various literary texts.

When scholars read chapters 52 and 53 of Isaiah using a canonical approach, they assume that it is a sacred, canonical, authoritative text. They might look at allusions in the chapters to earlier biblical traditions, especially those in Isaiah, and then at references to these chapters in later biblical texts. They might also trace the history of the text's interpretation, focusing perhaps on how the liturgical uses of these texts developed and affected theological reflection. Lastly, they would interpret the text as part of the canon as a whole.

## Exercise

Find all of the references to Isaiah used by New Testament writers. How are these writers interpreting the book of Isaiah? What assumptions do they make about the book of Isaiah? What aspects of Isaiah do they highlight? Are these important themes for Second Isaiah's (Isaiah 40 – 55) original audience, or is the New Testament author changing the meaning? How might these New Testament texts affect the ways that Christians read Isaiah?

## Liberation Theology and Postcolonialism

Liberation theology, which was initiated in the second half of the twentieth century by Catholic theologians from Latin America, has spread to many different countries and religions, including Judaism. One of the central ideas of liberation theology is that God opposes all aspects of human oppression; it seeks to realize here on earth the belief that all people are created with equal dignity and worth. Liberation theologians can point to many biblical texts that depict God as one who fights for the oppressed.

When liberation theology first arose, it was a response to Christians who economically oppressed fellow Christians without recognizing that they were doing so. Some Latin American liberation theologians have pointed out the Catholic Church's complicity in this oppression. In addition, some liberation theologians use Marxist economic theory to critique the Catholic Church. These Marxist elements led Christian churches at first to be wary of liberation theology. Today, however, Christian churches have begun to recognize their own complicity in supporting oppressive structures, even if it has often been unintentional. This has led many Christian denominations, including Catholicism, to accept liberation theology. Post-Holocaust theology is one example of the recognition that Christian theology can and has been used in the service of violence and oppression.

More broadly, liberation theology is an example of postcolonial interpretation. Colonialism is a complex process, so what follows is only a brief explanation. Following the age of discovery when Columbus landed in the Americas, European political and economic interests led to an expansion of European colonies throughout the world. By the middle of the twentieth century, the United States was also a colonizing power because many of its economic resources came from areas that were economically dependent on the United States. This political and economic dominance was coupled with cultural hegemony, or the cultural domination of one group over another. Colonized areas took on the cultural norms and values of their colonizers, even to the detriment of their own indigenous, or native, cultures.

Following the two World Wars, European influence began to wane (although U.S. influence increased). As countries in Africa, Asia, and Latin America became increasingly independent, their populations began to question the cultural norms that they had assumed as the result of colonization. We have seen a push to recover the cultural influences of native peoples and to reject any remnants of the culture of the colonizers to create new cultural identities. Within Latin American theology, for example, liberation theology seeks to create a Christian theology of *base communities*, that is, communities of the poor who suffer the effects of economic oppression yet still believe in a biblical God who liberates them from oppression.

Liberation theology, like the other approaches discussed in part 3, is not a monolithic entity. Different scholars use this approach to highlight different things. What is held in common in liberation approaches, however, are its ultimate aims, which are twofold. First, it aims to favor interpretations that lead to the annihilation of oppression in all of its forms. It does not seek to replace the domination of one group with that of another, but rather to resist all forms of domination to create a world where all people are treated with equal dignity. Second, while it recognizes that such a utopia can only be fully realized with the coming of the kingdom of God, it rejects any notion that the struggle against oppression in this world is irrelevant. Instead it advocates Jewish and Christian solidarity with the poor, and resistance to structures of political, economic, and cultural oppression.

In biblical studies, one example of this approach has centered on interpretations of the book of Exodus, as well as Jesus' interactions with the poor and marginalized. While many liberation theologians view God's rescue of the Israelites from slavery in Egypt as paradigmatic for God's care for the poor of the world, other groups who have experienced invasion, colonization, or other acts of conquest point out that the Exodus involved not just freedom from slavery but also possession of a land, which displaced the Canaanites. As a result of this biblical narrative, during the settlement of the United States, some Christians of European descent felt justified in displacing and annihilating people who were settled in a land that they believed was theirs by divine right. As the Native American theologian Robert Warrior points out in "Native American Perspective," one group's liberation may be another group's oppression.

Readings that are expressly liberationist take seriously the effect that an interpretation has had or will have on oppressed groups. Liberationists would reject an interpretation as valid if it condones, promotes, or justifies such oppression, even if that reading is historically accurate. While postcolonialism points out the oppressive attitudes that are inherent in some biblical texts, liberation theology goes beyond that, calling for the repudiation of these attitudes based on the theological principle of the inherent dignity of every human person.

## Exercise

Read interpretations of a single biblical passage, like the stories of the Exodus from Egypt or the descriptions of the suffering of Job, from a variety of liberation perspectives. For example, try to find scholars from Asia, Africa, and Latin America who identify themselves as using liberation theology. What do these interpretations have in common? What makes them different?

## CONTEXTUAL APPROACHES

One element of historical research that has long been recognized is that the cultural context of the historian affects what scholars notice, what they deem as important, and how they explain what they discover. For example, the increase of women in an academic field such as history has led to an increased awareness of the role women have played in all eras of human history.

Sometimes being a member of an oppressed group also makes one aware of how certain biblical texts have been used for both good and ill. The biblical slave laws are a case in point. As a white Christian, I was content to dismiss the laws permitting slavery in ancient Israel as an historical curiosity. To me it was something that was "okay back then." It wasn't until I began reading African American biblical scholars that I became aware of the use of these laws (and other biblical texts) by Christian slave owners in the nineteenth century to justify the owning of slaves.

While gender and race are important lenses through which to look at the Bible, social class also informs an interpreter's context. Traditionally biblical scholars came from the elite classes. If we think about the society of rich males of the late nineteenth and early twentieth centuries, we can understand that some of the elite perspectives of Israelite proverbs might sound like universal truths to them. For example, the description of the ideal wife in Proverbs 31, which opens with the warning, "Do not give your strength to women" (v. 3), characterizes this wife as diligent, resourceful, charitable, wise, and pious. What elite scholars failed to notice is that she is also rich, married, and works only to increase her husband's wealth. It has been the entry of various social classes into academia that has furthered our understanding of the economic location of the authors of these proverbs.

A contextual approach covers any criticism that makes use of the context of the interpreter as an important element in biblical interpretation. The aims of the contextual approach often include the following:

* highlighting overlooked elements in the text
* reading the text from the perspective of those oppressed within the text
* uncovering the use (or misuse) of the text by those in power to maintain a system of oppression (this often includes uncovering how the context of privilege has affected these interpretations)
* providing reading strategies for oppressed groups both to identify oppressive elements in a text and to counteract those elements

Often contextual approaches can be expressly theological in that they are interested in the meaning and use of the Bible today.

In Christian circles, contextual approaches have been especially prominent among ethnically diverse communities. These readings are explicitly theological because they arise out of the awareness that religious affiliation alone does not unify various Christian denominations. Peoples in Africa, for example, who have grown up in communities with tribal traditions experience the narratives of the patriarchs through the lens of their tribal experience. These readings can be at odds with readings from European and North American scholars, even if they share the same religion.

One of the fruits of a more ethnically diverse community of scholars is the recognition that often the social location of U.S. biblical scholars (highly educated from a globally dominant country) often makes them the least able to appreciate the social world of the biblical authors and their audience. Peoples from colonized countries, economically impoverished and struggling to maintain their dignity and identity, can often shed light on texts that U.S. scholars can miss.

All interpreters ought to engage in contextual approaches, because they make interpreters aware of their own bias. In addition, contextual approaches offer new readings of the text that any one individual perspective may have missed.

## Exercise

Look up passages in Proverbs that deal with the poor and loss of wealth. Would someone who was poor have written the same proverbs? What kinds of proverbs might slaves, for instance, have passed on to their children? How would they differ from those preserved in Proverbs?

## Feminist Hermeneutics

Feminist hermeneutics is an example of a contextual approach. The emergence of feminist hermeneutics is one example of how changes in the demographics of scholarship have filled out research on biblical history and broadened awareness of the effect of interpretation on the contemporary world. Like any interpretation from a cultural perspective, feminist hermeneutics is multifaceted. Not all feminists think the same way, just as not all males have the same perspective. But one finds three major branches in feminist interpretations of the Bible:

- **Historical and literary recovery.** Some feminist interpretations seek to recover the important role women play in the Bible. Sometimes this recovery focuses on historical questions: What role did women play in the royal court? in the family? in religion? Sometimes scholars focus on the literary characters often overlooked in traditional interpretations; this sometimes means reading from the perspective of unnamed and silent characters. This work of recovery has led to a fuller and more accurate picture of the world of the biblical text.

- **Decentering the question of meaning.** For a long time, women were told that their readings of the Bible were "wrong" because they did not always match the interpretation of male scholars. Feminists challenge claims of a text's male-oriented "objective" meaning by showing how those claims support a system of patriarchy. Patriarchy is used to refer to a hierarchical social structure where only a small segment of the male population has unearned privileges. In North America, this segment includes a small group of elite, white, heterosexual males. The rest of society is structured to support and enable this power structure. Feminist scholarship challenges the patriarchal ideology that both produced the text and authorizes interpretations.

- **The danger of interpretation.** Feminists have also made scholars more aware of the effects of biblical interpretation on the lives of women, especially in societies dominated by Christianity. Some feminist scholars trace the impact of a particular interpretation on women. The interpretation of Genesis 3:16, "Your desire shall be for your husband, and he shall rule over you," as a universal command rather than a curse within a particular piece of literature, for example, has reinforced women's legal subordination to men throughout much of Christian history.

Sometimes people blame feminism for the discomfort that comes when unrecognized biases are revealed. However, movements such as feminist hermeneutics simply remind us of realities that Christian interpreters have known since the Church began: that interpretation is always a complex process; that "meaning" in a text always encompasses a range of possibilities (called layers of meaning); that interpretation should always be a communal process; and that a lot is at stake whenever anyone interprets the Bible because of its authority for many communities of faith.

## Exercise

Read either the story of David and Bathsheba in 2 Samuel 11 or the story of the woman at the well in John 4. What assumptions does the text make about the role of women in their society and about the relationship of women to God? Would the story be different if it was told from the perspective of the female character? Look at historical artwork of the story: how is the main female character portrayed in this artwork, and what does that suggest about how women have been viewed by various reading communities?

## Materialist Readings

Although race and gender have been recognized as lenses through which we read the text, economic and class issues have remained more invisible. While liberation theologians and postcolonial scholars have pointed out how biblical interpretations have supported the ongoing economic exploitation of the developing world, classism has only recently become a lens through which to view the biblical text in a sustained way.

Like the other approaches described in part 3, a materialist reading of the text first aims to uncover the economic parameters that shaped the text's production and ideology. For example, feminist scholars, like Carol Meyers and Gale Yee, have researched women's functions in the ancient Israelite economy to explain how biblical portrayals of women often stem from anxiety in the ancient world over women's important role in the ancient economy through their contributions to family farming and other household businesses. A materialist reading of a text like Genesis 3:16 interprets God's curse of Eve as reflecting women's high death rates in childbirth, even though one of the most important things women did for the family was give birth to the next generation, who were needed to continue the work of the family farm.

Materialist readings also describe how certain interpretations of biblical texts have addressed contemporary economic interests. A clear example is the way that Christian slave owners in the nineteenth century interpreted certain biblical texts in a way that justified the practice of slavery that was necessary for them to maintain their economic status as plantation owners.

Materialist readings note the complexity of social status in an Israelite society colonized by Persia, Greece, and Rome. Within these empires, Judean men who reached a kind of elite status did so only by cooperating with the imperial ruling power. By using cross-cultural studies and economic theories, materialist readings uncover the ways that Judean elites coped within a system of economic oppression. These studies show that fights over who could control the temple in the Persian period or questions over who could interpret the law in the Roman period functioned within a complex web of imperial economic control. The Sadducees in the time of Jesus, for example, although religious leaders within Judea, held what little power they had only by cooperation with the Roman government.

These studies remind scholars that biblical texts were often addressed to people struggling for identity and survival within a context of colonization. This realization undercuts the attempt of elites within modern society to identify themselves as the marginalized peoples with whom Jesus interacted, or with the oppressed people who enjoyed God's destruction of the wicked. Instead it asks economically privileged readers of the Bible to examine their relationship to poor people in today's world.

## Exercise

Read the parable of Lazarus and the rich man in Luke 16:19 – 31. What is the parable's attitude toward wealth and poverty? Can you find other places in the Gospel of Luke that share this attitude?

## CULTURAL CRITICISM

Cultural criticism is an approach that was first developed by scholars of literature and quickly spread to art, music, and theology. Like many of the movements surveyed in this part of the book, it can mean different things to different scholars. I will not attempt to do justice to its multifaceted manifestations. Instead, I will provide a brief introduction.

One of the first things that cultural criticism does is examine what communities mean by "culture." In spite of its name, this is not a method that surveys items that most people view as culture. Instead, it examines the variety of ways that a given culture is created, maintained, and develops. Its particular interest is in the "unofficial" or noncontrollable vehicles for cultural expression: street art, popular music, paperback novels, sitcoms on television, and so on.

The aims of this approach are twofold and interrelated. First, this focus undercuts the hegemony or monopolization of culture by the privileged and elite in a community. It questions their authority to determine what is "art" or "culture." Second, it makes room for cultural expressions that are usually not the subject of elite study, expressions that are often highly influential on large groups of people. For example, racial and ethnic groups have questioned the ongoing omission of their art and music from the cultural canon because, for some reason, these works have been denigrated as "popular," "unschooled," or "low" culture.

These aims align cultural criticism with deconstructionism. Cultural criticism seeks to deconstruct the authority that certain evaluations of culture have had in order to bring in voices often silenced by that authorizing process. It is also thoroughly postmodern because it gives voice to a variety of communities who have often been left out of the scholarly or cultural record.

In biblical studies, a variety of interpretations have been designated as cultural criticism. Some ethnic scholars would view their work, not as liberationist, but as using a cultural approach. This is most clearly seen when the goal is to introduce the interpretations of those in their community who have not had access to higher education. For example, some Latin American biblical scholars have shown how the book of Exodus has been important among the poor in their understanding of the biblical message of liberation. Similarly, African American biblical scholars have shown how biblically based spirituals not only came out of the cultural context of American slavery, but continue to inform the cultural world of contemporary African American Christians.

Other scholars have looked at American popular culture for examples of interpretive traditions. A number of scholars have looked at the role that film has had as both a vehicle of interpretation and as a reflection of the ways popular culture interprets the Bible. Others have examined music, television, or popular novels as vehicles for biblical interpretation.

These studies argue that the disconnection that often exists between the interpretations of biblical scholars and what most people think about the Bible is the result of much greater social forces than is often recognized. They urge biblical scholars to engage popular culture more vigorously if they want their interpretations to have an effect on American culture.

## Exercise

Take a biblical figure, like King David, Moses, or Jesus, and find three films that depict this figure. What do these films assume about the audience's attitude toward the Bible? Do these films veer away from the biblical text? When and why? How might each film influence the audience's interpretation of this biblical figure?

# PART 4

## THE HISTORY
## OF BIBLICAL
## INTERPRETATON

One new movement within the field of biblical interpretation is an increased interest in the history of the interpretation of a particular text. There are many reasons for this renewed interest, and each of these reasons affects both the material that is reviewed and the treatment of that material. Because this is such a new field, however, many scholars are unaware of the variety of purposes that it can serve.

Some of the most prominent approaches to the history of interpretation focus on the work of "recovery." This approach can sometimes be coupled with a negative attitude toward contemporary methods of biblical interpretation. Precritical interpretations, meaning those dating before the Enlightenment, are usually privileged, and within those the goal is to uncover the dominant interpretations, especially those that have had the most influence on denominational teachings. This approach tends to focus on interpretations within larger theological treatises or sermons.

This, however, is only one reason that the history of interpretation is important. Alternatively, some biblical scholars have used the interpretation of the text as a way to reveal where persistent difficulties in the text lie. By looking at sticking points in interpretation across a wide variety of time periods, the problematic or ambiguous nature of the text becomes more apparent. This approach uses history as a way to see the biblical text better. This approach often focuses on formal treatises of biblical interpretation, such as commentaries, since that is where scholars usually delve deeper into the technical aspects of the text.

Others have looked at the text's interpretive history to uncover the cultural context of contemporary interpretation. For example, most Christians assume that the story of Adam and Eve is about the Fall and original sin, even though those terms do not appear in the account. Many of my students are surprised to learn that Jews do not have the same interpretation as Christians. My students were not aware that their assumptions about the text are the result of a long history of Christian interpretation of this material. Some scholars using this approach want to find ways to resist a given interpretation. The first step to resisting an interpretation, or at least relativizing it, is to set it as one option among several. Scholars explore the way that the historical context of the interpreter affects interpretation.

Still other scholars have focused on the interpretation of the biblical text in other media, such as literature, painting, music, and so on. While early attempts to trace the influence of the Bible centered on traditional theological texts, such as commentaries, sermons, and theological treatises, this more recent approach has shown that it is often artistic expressions that have a greater influence on popular culture. These scholars often use nontraditional material to demonstrate an interpretation's influence.

Tracing the history of biblical interpretation is a massive project, one usually requiring skills from across various academic disciplines. This final part of the book does not intend to teach students how to trace the history of a text's interpretation. Instead, it offers a few influential examples of traditional interpretations to illustrate the method. I have found it is easier to ask students to view artistic renderings of select biblical texts than it is to trace a text's interpretation in literature or theological writing. I have included three exercises appropriate for undergraduate students at the end of this section, each dealing with different sources for engaging the history of biblical interpretation. Whether texts or art are examined, students find it useful to understand the sources for some commonly held interpretations of influential biblical texts.

## THE VISIONS OF EZEKIEL
## AND CHRISTIAN THEOLOGY

Although the book of Ezekiel may not be widely read today, that has not been true for most of Christian history. Ezekiel's visions, in particular, were continually reused by Christian communities. For example, the vision of the dry bones was an important symbol of hope for slaves in the United States. The descriptions of the temple in the final chapters of the book were used by early missionaries to Central America, where the indigenous populations used similar sacred spaces to worship their gods.

The chariot-throne vision was an important image in both Jewish and Christian interpretation. Jewish exegesis used the chariot-throne image within its mystical traditions, including a movement called *kabbalah*. Christians read the vision as an allegory or symbolic picture of the Bible itself. This interpretation has two parts:

- In the first part, the four cherubim represent four sections of the Old Testament (as organized in the Septuagint and the Vulgate) and four corresponding sections of the New Testament:

| Law | Gospels |
|---|---|
| History | Acts of the Apostles |
| Wisdom | Epistles |
| Prophecy | Revelation |

- In the second part, the four faces are symbols of the four Gospel writers (sometimes these four symbols are depicted with wings to connect them more closely with the cherubim in Ezekiel's vision):

| Man or angel | Matthew |
|---|---|
| Lion | Mark |
| Ox | Luke |
| Eagle | John |

Another of Ezekiel's visions that became especially important for Catholics is the vision of the locked door in Ezekiel 44. Early Christian interpreters saw this as a symbol of Mary, the mother of Jesus. Just as the temple was God's dwelling on earth, Mary was a temple housing God in the form of Jesus. In some paintings of Gabriel's annunciation to Mary, a small temple in the background expresses her role as the temple of Jesus.

When God entered the temple in Ezekiel's vision, God permanently locked the door of the temple. Similarly, Catholic theologians explaining the doctrine of Mary's perpetual virginity noted that God made Mary's womb a dwelling for Jesus, "locking" it behind him. The Old Testament image highlights that this Catholic teaching is actually a way to emphasize the divine nature of Jesus.

## ISAIAH'S SUFFERING SERVANT, JESUS, AND THE "DOUBLE LITERAL"

Chapters 40 – 55 of the book of Isaiah contain a series of poems describing a servant of God who suffered for the sins of others. Many Christians would assert that Jesus is this Suffering Servant predicted by the prophet Isaiah. But is that the only meaning of the text? Did a Jewish community preserve this text for more than five hundred years not knowing what it meant? Most biblical scholars would assert that the text had a different function in its original context. The question for contemporary theologians, then, is what is the relationship of the text's original meaning to this later Christian reinterpretation?

Any introduction to the book of Isaiah lays out the options for the text's meaning in its original context. The writer of Second Isaiah used the image of the Suffering Servant to symbolize some particular person or group, such as a future ruler or ruling family, who he felt did not deserve to suffer through the long exile. Since these texts are metaphors, they have a "surplus of meaning," which means that the symbol can have meanings on different levels to different groups.

These passages also have an element of ambiguity. The poems never present a consistent designation of who or what the Suffering

Servant was meant to represent. In addition, the promises of an idyllic restoration that the servant would see were never fully realized. This meant that these beautifully crafted poems piqued the imagination of the communities of Jews and later Christians who read these as scripture.

By the time the texts in the New Testament were written, many Jews read prophetic texts as referring to future events; this is common in the Dead Sea Scrolls. After Jesus suffered and died on the cross, early Christians found in Second Isaiah a way to make sense of Jesus' horrible death.

Most Christians assume that the Gospels quote these poems often, especially when they describe Jesus' death, but only a few direct quotations from Second Isaiah appear in the New Testament. The most direct quote is found in Matthew 8:17, where it explains why Jesus spent so much time healing people: "This was to fulfill what had been spoken through the prophet Isaiah, 'He took our infirmities and bore our diseases.'" The connection between the Suffering Servant and Jesus' death on the cross is most clearly made in a later text, 1 Peter 2:22 – 25. Christian postbiblical tradition made the most of these links. From an early period, texts from Isaiah have been included in the liturgy at Advent and Lent.

So in what way is the Suffering Servant Jesus? Nicholas of Lyra in the fourteenth century provided the Church with a helpful way to think about this problem. He introduced the notion of a "double literal" sense. Texts in the Old Testament have their own literal meaning. But when Old Testament texts are quoted in the New Testament, they take on an additional literal meaning that fits that literary context.

- The literal meaning of the Suffering Servant when read exclusively in the context of the book of Isaiah is possibly that of a royal figure or group.
- The literal meaning of the Suffering Servant in Matthew 8:17 and 1 Peter 2:22 – 25 is that he is Jesus, the Christ.

Therefore, for Christians, the Suffering Servant is both a royal person or group in the Restoration period and Jesus Christ: the figure has two literal meanings.

This way of reading avoids the heresy of *supercessionism*. Supercessionism involves the assertion that the original meaning of the text is superseded or nullified by the later meaning. A supercessionist reading of the Suffering Servant would say that although the Israelites thought this poem was about a figure in the past, we know that it is exclusively about Jesus.

Recently instead of supercessionism, some Catholic theologians have talked about a *sensus plenior*. This phrase is translated as the "fuller sense" of the text, and it is a shorthand way to say that a text can have multiple meanings. Although this is a term found more often in Catholic theology, it expresses an idea common in many Christian denominations. Throughout most of Christian history, biblical exegetes have talked about the text as having multiple meanings. By the high Middle Ages, Christian theologians concluded that every text has a literal meaning, but they also realized texts can mean more than one thing. The Suffering Servant is a case in point. The literal meaning is set in the context of the period of the late Exile. The Servant as Christ, however, is an additional, or "fuller," meaning of the text.

Many Christians would hold that the Suffering Servant refers to a figure at the time of the late Exile and to Christ. Both meanings are part of the divine revelation of the text, and neither is less "holy" or canonical, although the literal meaning in both contexts is what must be affirmed.

## JEWISH-CHRISTIAN RELATIONS AND THE EFFECTS OF INTERPRETATION

Not all of the results of traditional Christian interpretations of biblical texts have been positive. The belief that Isaiah 7:14 predicts the virgin birth of Jesus is one such case. Notice that in the context of the book of Isaiah, this passage is not about the woman at all. The woman and her child are merely a literary device to mark off time in the oracle.

The assumption that this text refers to Mary comes from a text-critical problem. The Hebrew text identifies the woman as a "young woman." It is the Septuagint that translates the word as "virgin."

Matthew 1:23, reading with the Septuagint, states that this verse is "fulfilled" in Mary's conception of Jesus. Christians can debate what the author of Matthew 1:23 meant by that text, but that is a separate question from the meaning of the text in the book of Isaiah.

The problem for Christians comes with the assumption that Isaiah 7:14 has only one meaning, and that all other claims to what it signifies are wrong. This is exactly what happened in the Middle Ages. Christians believed that this text was so obviously about Jesus that anyone who would deny it must be evil, stubborn, or obstinate.

The few Christian scholars able to read Hebrew in the Middle Ages realized that the Hebrew text does not contain the word *virgin*. Some of them asserted that Jews must have changed the original wording of the text, which was faithfully preserved in the Septuagint. Jewish leaders, they posited, changed the Scriptures so that their people would not convert to Christianity upon realizing that Jesus was predicted in their own Scriptures.

These debates about Isaiah 7:14 took place in a world of increasing hostility of Christians to both Jews and Muslims. In the High Middle Ages, Christians, under the direction of the papacy, burned Jewish books and translations. They justified this violence by saying that these books were keeping Jews from converting to Christianity. It was not a great leap from this violence against Jewish property to violence against Jewish persons. As efforts to convert Jews increased, so too did violence against them when those efforts failed.

This justification of violence is a sad element of the Christian tradition. Adding to the tragedy is that with the discoveries of ancient biblical texts found at Qumran, we now know that "young woman" is the original wording of the passage in Isaiah.

The history of biblical interpretation has led Christian scholars to ask: What is Christianity's responsibility when biblical interpretations lead to injustice, oppression, and especially violence? This is not just a problem with this text. Interpretations of the slave laws or the curse of Ham in Genesis 9:25 – 27, for example, are other examples of interpretations that have led to violence and injustice. Can a church affirm an interpretation of the Bible as "correct" while ignoring the effects of that interpretation? Should some interpretations be viewed as "wrong" not because they are theoretically impossible, but because they are too easily misused?

# GENDER, GOD,
# AND THE CHRISTIAN TRADITION

Many people today picture God as a wise old man with white hair and a beard, a picture based, in part, on the description of God in Daniel 7:9. Although it is Christian belief that Christ became a man when he was here on earth, Christians also believe that God does not have a body, so God cannot literally be a man.

Christian theologians, such as Thomas Aquinas, have long noted that all language about God is metaphorical. God is so far beyond human comprehension, and our human language is so limited, that anything humans say about God only approximates the reality of God's essence.

The Bible uses many human metaphors for God, and many of these are male metaphors. For instance, in calling God the husband of Jerusalem, the author is using a clear male image. When Jesus says to call God "Father," he is also using a male metaphor. In many of Jesus' parables about the kingdom, the figure that represents God is a male, like the father of the prodigal son.

Sometimes, however, the Bible uses female images to describe God. For instance, Deuteronomy 32:11 – 13 uses images of a mother bird and a nursing mother to describe God's care for Israel. Similarly, Hosea 11:4 describes God as a nursing mother bending down to feed her child. Occasionally Jesus uses a female metaphor for God, such as in the parable of the woman searching for a lost coin (Luke 15:8 – 10).

The most enduring female image for God is Wisdom. In much of the proverbial literature, Wisdom is an aspect of God's work in creation. Wisdom of Solomon 7:25 states this explicitly, "[Wisdom] is a breath of the power of God, and a pure emanation of the glory of the Almighty." Wisdom is consistently personified as a woman throughout the Wisdom literature. This female figure helps God in creating and sustaining the universe, and in maintaining order and balance in the world. The use of both male and female images for God in the Old Testament is one way the Israelites affirmed that these images are metaphors. God is not literally male or female.

When Christian theologians think of Jesus, they recognize that Jesus was a man with a male body. But they also recognize Jesus as Christ as both fully human (and literally male) as well as fully divine (neither male nor female). The New Testament affirms that the divine aspect of Christ is also not literally male when it equates Christ with Wisdom. The beginning of John's Gospel, for instance, uses descriptions of Lady Wisdom from Proverbs and Wisdom to describe Christ as God's "Word." Colossians 1:15 – 20 also uses language of Lady Wisdom to praise Christ, depicting the involvement of Wisdom/Christ in creation.

Christian mystics have maintained the use of male and female images of God, Christ, and the Holy Spirit as a way to penetrate the mystery of God's nature. For example, Julian of Norwich, a mystic from the fifteenth century, had visions of Christ as mother. Therefore, while Jesus states that his followers can address God in prayer as "Our Father," neither Jesus nor later Christian tradition claims that this is the only way one can address God. Both Scripture and tradition affirm that female metaphors, such as Mother and Lady Wisdom, can be applied to all three persons of the Trinity: God, Christ, and the Holy Spirit.

Many contemporary Christian communities are involved in the revitalization of this multi-gendered tradition. Some communities pray to God as both father and mother. Artists have depicted the crucified Jesus with a female body, just as Chinese artists have depicted him as Chinese, Native Americans have depicted him with indigenous elements, and so on. These artists are communicating that Jesus died for the sins of all humanity, not just for those whose bodies resembled his. Theologians have noted the importance of nurturing metaphors for God as a counterbalance to images of power and military might. These interpretations are not new, but carry on a biblical and interpretive tradition that has always been a part of Christianity.

## THE SIGN OF JONAH AND THE ARTISTIC TRADITION

When most people think about Jonah, they picture the prophet sitting in the belly of a whale. Yet most Old Testament scholars would assert that this event is not the central part of the book. Why is there such a divide between popular opinion and professional conclusions?

There are two interrelated reasons: the use of Jonah in the New Testament and the portrayal of the Jonah story by Christian artists.

Jonah is mentioned twice in the New Testament (Matt 12:38 – 42 and Luke 11:29 – 32). In these texts, Jonah's three-day sojourn in the belly of the fish is used to foreshadow Jesus' three-day stay in the tomb. This is referred to as the sign of Jonah. In the book of Jonah, the prayer of the prophet likens his time in the belly of the fish to being in the clutches of death. For Christians, the story of Jonah's flight from God's command to prophesy to Nineveh provided an opportunity for this prophet to become a "type of Christ." He suffered in a kind of "tomb" before his mission to the Gentiles was realized.

Artistic images of Jonah play with this dual interpretation of the prophet. Many depict Jonah as a kind of Christ figure, some using crosses, light, or other elements associated with Jesus. Early Christian paintings depict the fish as a chaos monster, such as Leviathan; these versions try to convey the cosmic nature of Jonah's struggle as a prefiguration of Christ's victory over sin and chaos.

These artistic renderings illustrate the Christian notion of *typology*. Typology was popular in the patristic era. Early Christian exegetes viewed much of the Old Testament material as providing "types," or prefigurations of Jesus. This differs from allegory because an allegory is a metaphor or symbol that has no existence on its own. When Paul says that Sarah is an allegory for those free from the law in Galatians, he is claiming Sarah as a symbol, not as a real, living person.

Typology, on the other hand, presumes the existence of the person, event, or item in history that prefigures what will come later. Jonah as a "type" of Christ affirms the existence of an historical Jonah who had meaning within his own historical time period. It simply asserts that the ultimate purpose of Jonah's existence was not the mission to the Ninevites, but is revealed in Jesus' three-day interment in the tomb. Both events mutually illuminate each other.

In popular culture, however, it has been the later meaning that has survived. Jonah's mission to the Ninevites and his stubborn refusal to rejoice at their salvation has been forgotten. Instead, Jonah is a man who God saves from the terrible fate of having been swallowed up by a big fish, a symbol of death. This "picture" of Jonah fills the collective imagination, an image promoted by countless artistic representations.

This use of artistic depictions of Jonah demonstrates that artistic pieces often combine images derived from the biblical text with a tradition of interpretation stemming from a variety of sources. In this case, it helps illuminate typological interpretation that has been influential within the Christian traditions of biblical interpretation. It also demonstrates that cultural appropriation of biblical and Christian traditions can become more powerful than the scriptural text itself.

## Exercises

1. One of the most enduring metaphors that Christians have used to describe the Church is that it is the "bride of Christ." Find both Old and New Testament texts that use the metaphor of God as the husband and Israel, Jerusalem, or the Church as the bride or wife. How does the Bible use this metaphor? Then find Christian texts from the patristic and medieval periods that use this metaphor. What biblical texts are these interpretations most dependent on? What biblical texts does this later use ignore or omit?

2. Many New Testament passages quote or use Old Testament passages. One example is the quotation of Isaiah 40:3 to refer to John the Baptist in Matthew 3:3, Mark 1:3, Luke 3:4, and John 1:23. Compare Jewish and Christian interpretations of that Old Testament passage in three different eras: the patristic-rabbinic period, the Middle Ages, and the modern era. What do these interpretations have in common? How do they differ? Are they interacting with each other, or have they developed in isolation from each other?

3. Pick a particular biblical character or figure and find artistic images of that figure (painting, sculpture, church decoration, and so on) across various times and places. What elements of the biblical text are most highlighted in the artistic tradition? How do these images represent a particular interpretation of the text? What elements of the text do they ignore or omit?

# FOR FURTHER READING

Students can consult many guides to biblical interpretation to learn more about any of the methods described in this primer. Some guides deal with only a few methods, whereas others are more comprehensive. Some are theoretical, designed for scholars in the field, whereas others address a more general audience. Among some of the best are those found in the series published by Fortress Press called Guides to Biblical Scholarship. Following are just a few books that give more detailed descriptions of the biblical methods.

Adam, A. K. M., ed. *Handbook of Postmodern Biblical Interpretation.* Saint Louis: Chalice, 2000.

Anderson, Janice C., and Stephen D. Moore, eds. *Mark and Method: New Approaches in Biblical Studies.* Rev. ed. Minneapolis: Fortress, 2008.

Barton, John. *Reading the Old Testament: Method in Biblical Study.* Rev. ed. Louisville: Westminster John Knox, 1996.

Harrington, Daniel. *Interpreting the New Testament: A Practical Guide.* New Testament Message 1. Wilmington: Michael Glazier, 1979.

——. *Interpreting the Old Testament: A Practical Guide.* Old Testament Message 1. Wilmington: Michael Glazier, 1981.

Hayes, John H., and Carl R. Holladay. *Biblical Exegesis: A Beginner's Handbook.* 3rd ed. Louisville: Westminster John Knox, 2007.

McKenzie, Steven L., and Stephen R. Haynes, eds. *To Each Its Own Meaning: An Introduction to Biblical Criticisms and Their Applications.* Rev. ed. Louisville: Westminster John Knox, 1999.

Steck, Odil H. *Old Testament Exegesis: A Guide to the Methodology.* 2nd ed. Vol. 39 of Resources for Biblical Study. Atlanta: Scholars, 1998.

Stuart, Douglas. *Old Testament Exegesis: A Handbook for Students and Pastors.* 3rd ed. Louisville: Westminster John Knox, 2001.

Yee, Gale, ed. *Judges and Method: New Approaches in Biblical Studies.* Rev. ed. Minneapolis: Fortress, 2007.

## Works Cited

In a few places in this guidebook, I refer to the works of other scholars. The details of those references can be found here:

Childs, Brevard. *Biblical Theology of the Old and New Testaments: Theological Reflection on the Christian Bible.* Minneapolis: Fortress, 1993. See also his commentary on Isaiah in the Old Testament Library series.

Gunkel, Hermann. *The Folktale in the Old Testament. Historic Texts and Interpreters in Biblical Scholarship.* Sheffield: Almond, 1987; originally published in German in 1921.

Hayes, John H., ed. *The Dictionary of Biblical Interpretation.* Nashville: Abingdon, 1999.

Koehler, George E. *The United Methodist Member's Handbook.* Rev. ed. Discipleship Resources, 2006.

Meyers, Carol. *Discovering Eve: Ancient Israelite Women in Context.* New York: Oxford, 1991.

Pontifical Biblical Commission. "The Interpretation of the Bible in the Church." *Origins* 23.29 (Jan 6, 1994): 495 – 524.

Pritchard, James B., ed. *Ancient Near Eastern Texts Relating to the Old Testament with Supplement.* Princeton, NJ: Princeton University Press, 1969.

Soares-Prabhu, George. "Laughing at Idols: The Dark Side of Biblical Monotheism (an Indian Reading of Isaiah 44:9 – 20)." In *Reading from this Place*, vol. 2: *Social Location and Biblical Interpretation in Global Perspective*, ed. by Fernando F. Segovia and Mary Ann Tolbert. Minneapolis: Fortress, 1995.

Warrior, Robert Allen. "Native American Perspective: Canaanites, Cowboys, and Indians." In *Voices from the Margin: Interpreting the Bible in the Third World.* Rev. ed. Ed. by R. S. Sugirtharajah. Maryknoll: Orbis, 2006.

Wellhausen, Julius. *Prolegomena to the History of Ancient Israel.* New York: Meridian Books/World Publishing Company, 1961; originally published in German in 1878.

Yee, Gale. *Poor Banished Children of Eve: Woman as Evil in the Hebrew Bible.* Minneapolis: Fortress, 2003.

# INDEX